SPECTACULAR BUILDINGS
EDIFICES SPECTACULAIRES
SPEKTAKULÄRE GEBÄUDE

SPECTACULAR BUILDINGS
EDIFICES SPECTACULAIRES
SPEKTAKULÄRE GEBÄUDE

EVERGREEN

EVERGREEN is an imprint of
TASCHEN GmbH

© 2007 TASCHEN GmbH

Hohenzollernring 53, D-50672 Köln

www.taschen.com

Editor Editrice Redakteur:
Simone Schleifer

English translation Traduction anglaise Englische Übersetzung:
Matthew Clarke

French translation Traduction française Französische Übersetzung:
Marion Westerhoff

German translation Traduction allemande Deutsche Übersetzung:
Susanne Engler

Proof reading Relecture Korrektur:
Gene Ferber, Marie-Pierre Santamarina, Martin Rolshoven

Art director Direction artistique Art Direktor:
Mireia Casanovas Soley

Graphic design and layout Mise en page et maquette Graphische Gestaltung und Layout:
Elisabet Rodríguez, Laura Millán

Printed by Imprimé par Gedruckt durch:
Anman Gráficas del Vallés, Spain

ISBN: 978-3-8228-4217-1

Contents   Index   Inhalt

"Architecture is the most democratic of the arts, and the buildings that surround us, affect us at a deep level. For architecture to be truly spectacular, it has to lift the moods of the people who pass by it, who work within it, who see it on a skyline or at the end of a street.... they push our knowledge and understanding of architecture forward and stimulate and showcase new ideas." — RIBA (Royal Institute of British Architects)

Rather than merely fulfilling an aesthetic purpose, today's new buildings have cultural, political, and social importance, and only those that succeed in reflecting these values, in combination with a novel approach to the practice of architecture, can be considered as spectacular. Challenged by an increasingly complex urban context, the buildings must carefully integrate their designs into the existing urban fabric through a skillful and sensitive interpretation of the buildings' purpose and relationship with the public.

Ever since the launch of Frank Gehry's Guggenheim Museum in Bilbao, eye-catching, head-turning, and jaw-dropping buildings with curvy shapes, jagged edges, and flashy materials have followed suit and made the short lists for the world's most prestigious competitions. Even architects, known for their classic style, have joined in with extraordinary, fancy and curious designs. Regardless of whether these odd-looking buildings are considered to be true icons or merely sensationalistic examples of iconic architecture, there is no reason why they cannot embrace the best of both worlds and express underlying values through visually impressive design.

Bearing in mind these issues and criteria, this book gathers a selection of contemporary projects completed within the last few years that exemplify the latest trends in the creation of prominent institutional, corporate, retail, cultural and educational facilities around the world. Internationally praised for their contribution to the architectural field and their novel approach to building, these projects not only impress with their unique appearance, but also take into consideration the fundamental aspects of quality and context. Whether they are perceived as icons or as simply iconic, there is no doubt that each of the following buildings responds to the claim for beauty, firmness, and utility, having won the favor of the public and professionals alike. Challenging and informative, these strong designs by internationally renowned architects offer direction to the profession, as well as provide people and places with lasting icons that provoke sensations and stimulate an interactive dialogue between human beings and their physical environment.

L'architecture est le plus démocratique de tous les arts et les édifices qui nous entourent nous touchent au plus profond de nous-mêmes. Pour que l'architecture soit vraiment spectaculaire, elle doit enthousiasmer les gens qui passent, qui y travaillent, l'aperçoivent se profiler à l'horizon ou au bout d'une rue .... Les constructions spectaculaires subliment notre connaissance et compréhension de l'architecture, stimulent la création de nouvelles idées. — RIBA (Royal Institute of British Architects)

Plus que répondre uniquement à un but esthétique, les nouvelles constructions revêtent une importance culturelle, politique et sociale. Et seules celles qui parviennent à refléter ces valeurs, en les conjuguant à une approche innovatrice de l'architecture, peuvent être qualifiées de spectaculaires. Mis au défi par un contexte urbain complexe, les édifices doivent intégrer leurs designs dans le tissu urbain existant, par le biais d'une interprétation subtile et sensible de leurs objectifs et relation avec le public.

Depuis l'inauguration du Guggenheim Museum de Frank Gehry à Bilbao, d'autres bâtiments aux formes courbes, angles découpés et matériaux voyants qui attirent le regard, éblouissent et laissent bouche bée ont suivi dans son sillage etant été sélectionnés par les concours les plus prestigieux du monde. Même les architectes, réputés pour leur style classique, rejoignent les rangs, à coup de designs fabuleux, sophistiqués et insolites. Que ces édifices bizarres soient de véritables icônes ou tout simplement des exemples sensationnels d'architecture iconique, rien ne les empêche de retenir le meilleur des deux mondes pour exprimer des valeurs implicites par le biais de design à l'optique impressionnante.

Tenant compte de ces enjeux et critères, cet ouvrage rassemble une sélection de projets d'architecture contemporaine remarquables, réalisés dans le monde au cours de ces dernières années. Ces œuvres illustrent les ultimes tendances dans la création d'installations institutionnelles, corporatives, commerciales, culturelles et éducatives. Couverts d'éloges et reconnus internationalement pour leur contribution à l'architecture et leur approche novatrice de la construction, ces projets ne sont pas uniquement exceptionnels pour leur apparence unique, mais également, pour leur respect des critères essentiels, tels que la qualité et le contexte. Considérés comme icônes ou tout simplement iconiques, il ne fait aucun doute que les édifices présentés ici, qui ont déjà reçu les faveurs du public et des professionnels, répondent aux critères de beauté, solidité et utilité. Véritables gageures et sources d'informations, ces designs imposants, oeuvres d'architectes reconnus mondialement, aiguillent la profession sur de nouvelles voies, tout en offrant aux habitants et à leurs villes des icônes durables, qui déclenchent des sensations et stimulent un dialogue interactif entre les êtres humains et leur environnement physique.

 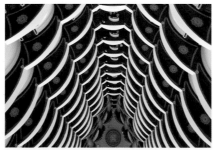  

„Die Architektur ist die demokratischste aller Künste, und die Gebäude, die uns umgeben, rufen starke Gefühle in uns hervor. Damit Architektur wirklich spektakulär wird, muss sie die Stimmung der Menschen beeinflussen, die an den Gebäuden vorbeigehen, die darin arbeiten, die sie am Horizont oder am Ende der Straße sehen. So wird unser Wissen um die Architektur immer größer und neue Ideen werden geboren und gezeigt." — RIBA (Royal Institute of British Architects)

Die neuen Gebäude der heutigen Zeit erfüllen nicht mehr einfach nur ästhetische Zwecke, sondern sie sind auch von kultureller, politischer und sozialer Bedeutung. Und nur die Gebäude, die diese Werte in Verbindung mit einer neuen Herangehensweise an das Konzept der Architektur zeigen, können als spektakulär betrachtet werden. Innerhalb eines immer komplexeren, städtischen Kontexts müssen neue Bauwerke so gestaltet sein, dass sie sich vorsichtig in die bestehende Stadtlandschaft einfügen. Dazu muss man den Zweck und die Beziehung der Gebäude zum Menschen mit Geschick und Einfühlungsvermögen interpretieren.

Seitdem Frank Gehry's Guggenheim Museum in Bilbao eingeweiht wurde, entstanden viele auffallende und erstaunliche Gebäude mit kurvigen Formen, zackigen Rändern und extravaganten Materialien. Sie alle kommen in die engere Wahl der auffallendsten und spektakulärsten Gebäude der Welt. Sogar Architekten, die für ihren klassischen Stil bekannt sind, haben sich mit außergewöhnlichen, phantasievollen und merkwürdigen Bauten an diesem Wettbewerb beteiligt. Ungeachtet dessen, ob man diese seltsamen Bauwerke als wirkliche Architekturikonen oder einfach nur als sensationalistische Beispiele für eine ikonische Architektur betrachtet, besteht kein Grund, warum sie nicht das Beste aus beiden Welten beinhalten und zugrunde liegende Werte durch eine visuell beeindruckende Gestaltung ausdrücken sollten.

Unter Berücksichtigung dieser Kriterien wurden in diesem Band Beispiele moderner Gebäude zusammengetragen, die in den letzten Jahren fertiggestellt wurden. Sie zeigen den neuesten architektonischen Trend: auffallende Gebäude, die von Institutionen, Unternehmen, dem Handel, Kultur- und Erziehungseinrichtungen geschaffen wurden. Sie werden auf internationaler Ebene für den Beitrag, den sie zur Architektur leisten, lobend erwähnt, und auch für die neue Herangehensweise an das Konzept eines Gebäudes. Diese Bauten beeindrucken nicht nur durch ihr einzigartiges Aussehen, sondern auch durch qualitative und kontextuelle Aspekte. Egal, ob man sie als Ikone oder einfach nur als ikonisch wahrnimmt, man muss jedem der im Folgenden gezeigten Bauwerke Schönheit, Beständigkeit und Nützlichkeit zugestehen; und jedes davon fand sowohl beim Publikum als auch in der Welt der Architektur großen Anklang. Diese auffallenden architektonischen Vorschläge international bekannter Architekten weisen dem Beruf eine neue Richtung. Sie stellen neue und beständige Ikonen für den Menschen und die Orte dar. Sie rufen Gefühle hervor und regen einen interaktiven Dialog zwischen dem Menschen und seiner physischen Umgebung an.

UFA Cinema Center

The UFA Cinema Center is conceived as an urban space, what is sustained through the softening of both the functional program and the building envelope to allow cultural functions to take place, and also through the injection of media events. The design is characterized by two intricately interconnected building units: the Cinema Block, with eight movie theaters and seating for 2,600, and the Crystal, a glass shell which serves simultaneously as foyer and public square. The interweaving of public squares, public interiors, and passageways was proposed as a way of energizing and densifying the new center of Dresden. The junctures between these urban vectors are defined as public spaces. The urban quality of the space is reinforced by circulation systems of stairs and bridges, which allow views of people through layers of light and color.

Le UFA Cinema Center, pensé comme un espace urbain, concept sous-jacent à la fois dans la programmation fonctionnelle et la structure de l'édifice, est conçu pour des évènements culturels, à l'instar des activités multimédia qui s'y déroulent. Le design affiche deux ensembles reliés de manière complexe : le bloc destiné au cinéma, doté de huit salles de projection avec une capacité d'accueil de 2.600 spectateurs et d'une salle tout en verre, servant à la fois de vestibule et de place publique. L'entrelacs de places publiques, d'intérieurs publics et de couloirs vise à dynamiser et densifier le nouveau centre de Dresde. Les liens entre ces nouveaux vecteurs urbains se définissent comme des espaces publics. Cette urbanité de l'espace est accentuée par un système de circulation composé de marches et de passerelles, offrant au visiteur une vision spatiale au travers de couches de lumière et couleurs.

Das dem UFA Cinema Center zugrunde liegende Konzept sieht die Schaffung eines städtischen Raums vor. Das zeigt sich sowohl in der Nutzung als auch am Baukörper, der für kulturelle Veranstaltungen und den Einsatz von darfür entwickelten Multimediasystemen entworfen wurde. Zwei Gebäude wurden auf auffallende Weise miteinander verbunden: ein Block mit acht Kinosälen für bis zu 2600 Zuschauer und ein Saal aus Glas, der die Funktion einer Vorhalle und eines öffentlichen Platzes verbindet. Die übernimmt verflechtung öffentlicher Plätze, Räume und Flure soll dieses neue Zentrum in Dresden dynamischer und dichter machen. Die Verbindungen zwischen diesen neuen städtischen Bauten wurden als öffentliche Räume definiert. Der positive Einfluss auf das Stadtbild wird durch die Treppen und Brücken, über die sich die Menschen bewegen, noch verstärkt, und der Betrachter sieht die Räume durch Schichten aus Licht und Farbe.

The diamond-shaped hall serves both as foyer and public square.

La salle de verre, en forme de diamant, peut être à la fois vestibule et place publique.

Der diamantförmige, verglaste Saal dient gleichzeitig als Vorhalle und als öffentlicher Platz.

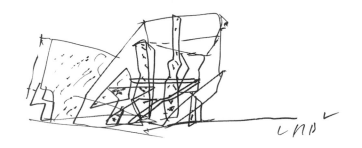

› Sketch Esquisse Skizze

Seattle Library

Bibliothèque de Seattle

Bibliothek von Seattle

The building is divided into eight horizontal layers, each varying in size to suit its function. A structural steel and glass skin unifies the multifaceted form and defines the public spaces in-between. The library is accessible from two different levels. Rows of escalators lead from the entrance level on 4th Street to the 5th Street lobby, located under a 50-foot-high sloping glass wall. The lobby can also be reached directly from a covered walkway than runs the length of the 5th Avenue façade. In order to the "combining" and consolidation of the apparently ungovernable proliferation of programs and media, five platforms were identified, each a programmatic cluster that is architecturally defined and equipped for maximum, dedicated performance. Because each platform is designed for a unique purpose, they are different in size, density and opacity.

L'édifice est divisé en huit étages horizontaux dont la dimension varie selon leur fonction. Une structure, à l'instar d'une « peau » d'acier et de verre, recouvre et définit les espaces publics qui s'y trouvent. L'accès à la bibliothèque est possible sur deux niveaux. Les escaliers mécaniques mènent de l'entrée de la Rue 4 au vestibule de la Rue 5, situé sous une paroi de verre inclinée de 15,24 m de haut. Il existe un deuxième accès par le passage couvert qui court le long de la façade dans la 5éme Avenue. Pour « réunir » et renforcer cette prolifération de programmes et d'éléments multimédia, incontrôlable, en apparence, cinq plateformes différentes ont été conçues, dotées chacune d'elle d'un groupe architectonique défini, équipé pour offrir un maximum de prestations. Chaque plateforme conçue dans un but différent varie en dimensions, densité et niveau d'opacité.

Das Gebäude unterteilt sich in acht Stockwerke, die je nach ihrer Funktion verschieden groß sind. Eine, wie eine Haut wirkende, Struktur aus Stahl und Glas verkleidet und definiert die öffentlichen Räume auf diesen Etagen. Man erreicht die Bibliothek auf zwei verschiedener Ebenen. Die Rolltreppen führen vom Eingang in der 4th Street zur Eingangshalle in der 5th Street, die sich unter einer schrägen, 15,24 m hohen Glaswand befindet. Ebenso erreicht man die Bibliothek über einen überdachten Gang, der an der Fassade der 5th Avenue entlang führt. Um diese anscheinend nicht beherrschbare Wucherung von Multimedialen Systemen und Funktionen in einen Zusammenhang zu bringen, schuf man fünf verschiedene Plattformen, von denen jede eine bestimmte architektonische Gruppe darstellt, die allen erforderten Funktionen entspricht. Da jede dieser Plattformen einem konkreten Zweck dient, unterscheiden sie sich in Abmessung, Dichte und Opazität.

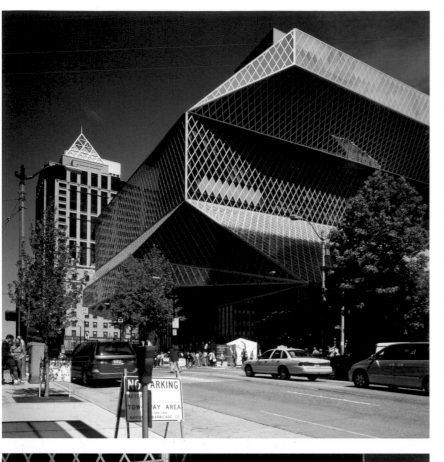

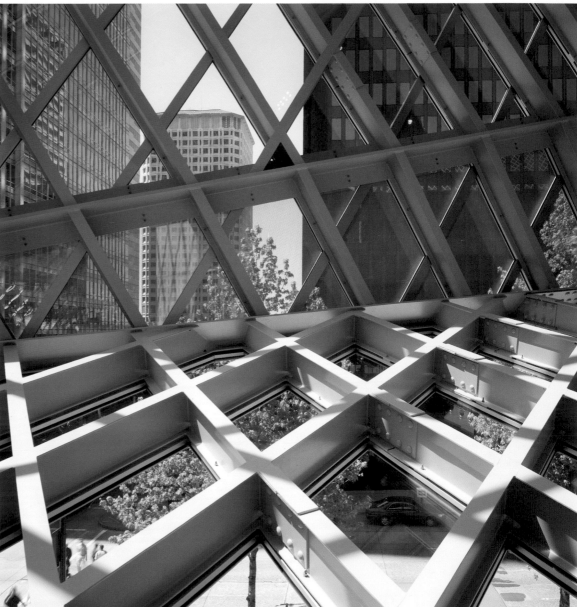

Casa da Música

OMA chose the historical center of the city to create a solitary building, standing on a new, intimate square, connected to the historical park of the 'Rotunda da Boavista' and enclosed by three urban blocks. Casa da Música is visually and spatially defined by its striking faceted exterior, from which its conventional interiors spaces have been extracted. The 15-inch-thick faceted shell is the main supporting element for the building's structural weight, working together with a system designed to maintain the stability of the horizontal parts of the shell while reinforcing the hall on the inside. A continuous ramp connects all the public elements to the various spaces located around the Grand Auditorium by means of steps, platforms and elevators, converting the building into a true architectural adventure. The 'loop' enables the building to be used for festivals holding simultaneous events.

Le OMA a choisi le centre historique de la ville pour héberger un édifice solitaire, implanté sur une nouvelle place en retrait, adjacente à la place historique de « Rotunda da Boavista » et entourée de trois blocs urbains. La Casa da Música se définit sur le plan visuel et spatial par un extérieur voyant, aux formes multiples, duquel émergent les espaces intérieurs. L'armature de l'édifice, d'une épaisseur de 40 cm, agit dans son ensemble en tant qu'élément principal de soutien du poids structural de l'édifice, supportant un système de stabilité qui maintient et unit les parties de l'armature à l'horizontale, tout en renforçant l'intérieur du vestibule. Une voie publique continue relie tous les éléments publics aux espaces restant situés autour du Grand Auditorium, par le biais de marches, plateformes et escaliers roulants : l'édifice se métamorphose alors en une véritable aventure architecturale. Le « loop » permet de l'utiliser pour des festivals aux présentations simultanées.

Das OMA wählte das historische Stadtzentrum für dieses einzigartige Gebäude ans. Es steht auf einem neuen, kleinen Platz an dem historischen Platz „Rotunda da Boavista" und ist umgeben von drei Häuserblöcken. Die Casa da Música fällt durch ungewöhnlich fassettierte äußere Formen auf, die den inneren Räumen entspringen. Das 40 cm dicke Gerüst des Gebäudes dient als tragendes Stützelement des Gewichtes der Gebäudestruktur. Das System, das Stabilität schafft, trägt und vereint die Teile des Gerüsts an der Längsseite und verstärkt außerdem das Innere der Eingangshalle. Ein durchgehender, öffentlicher Weg verbindet alle öffentlichen Elemente mit den übrigen Räumen, die sich um das große Auditorium befinden, über Treppen, Plattformen und Rolltreppen. Das Gebäude stellt ein architektonisches Abenteuer da. Das „Loop" bietet die Möglichkeit, das Gebäude für Festivals mit verschiedenen, gleichzeitig stattfindenden Aufführungen zu nutzen.

While from some perspectives the building presents an image of formal elegance, it appears remarkably unbalanced from some others.

Selon l'angle de vision, l'édifice peut revêtir une élégance presque formelle ou surprendre par son déséquilibre apparent.

Je nach Blickwinkel präsentiert sich das Gebäude in einer fast formalen Eleganz, während es aus anderen Perspektiven überraschend unausgewogen wirkt.

The hall, with room for 1,300 people, is a rehearsal space and houses the recording studios of the Porto National Orchestra.

La salle, dotée d'une capacité d'accueil de 1300 personnes, est un espace de répétition qui héberge aussi les studios d'enregistrement de l'Orchestre National de Porto.

Der Saal für 1300 Personen dient den Proben und beherbergt die Aufnahmestudios des Nationalorchesters von Porto.

Denver Art Museum Extension
Agrandissement du Denver Art Museum
Erweiterung des Denver Art Museums

This extension to the Denver Art Museum was added to the pre-existing building dating from 1971. Despite forming part of the same institution, the two entities were treated as two distinct constructions and even as two separate museums, connected by a steel-and-glass bridge. To reflect the connection between tradition and modernity, the new building used local stone and granite along with innovative materials like titanium. The extension has become the main entrance, reached via the 120-ft-high Pomar Grand Atrium, where a large staircase leads to the exhibition galleries. The constantly changing light, atmospheric effects and variable climate typical of Denver posed great challenges in the construction of the building, and its façade changes color and appearance according to the sunlight and the position of the onlooker.

L'agrandissement du Musée d'Art de Denver est une extension du musée déjà existant, conçu en 1971. Tout en formant une même entité, ces deux volumes sont sur le plan architectural deux édifices différents et même deux musées séparés, reliés par une passerelle en verre et acier. Pour rehausser le lien entre tradition de la construction existante et modernité du nouvel édifice, la pierre locale et le granit côtoient de nouveaux matériaux comme le titane. L'agrandissement concerne l'entrée principale, à laquelle on accède par le Pomar Grand Atrium, de 37 m de haut, d'où part un grand escalier desservant les galeries d'exposition. Les fluctuations constantes de lumière, les effets atmosphériques et les changements climatiques propres à Denver ont été les principaux défis à résoudre pour construire l'édifice dont la façade change de teintes et d'apparence en fonction de la lumière du jour et l'angle de perception du visiteur.

Die Erweiterung des Denver Art Museums ist ein Museumsanbau aus dem Jahr 1971. Obwohl beide Gebäude zur gleichen Körperschaft gehören, wurden sie architektonisch wie zwei verschiedene Bauten und sogar wie zwei getrennte Museen behandelt, die durch eine Tür aus Stahl und Glas miteinander verbunden sind. Um die Verbindung der Tradition mit der Modernität deutlich zu machen, benutzte man an dem neuen Gebäude Naturstein aus der Region und Granit kombiniert mit neuen Materialien wie Titan. Dieser Anbau ist der neue Haupteingang, erreichbar über das Pomar Grand Atrium auf 37 m Höhe. Hier führt eine große Treppe zu den Ausstellungsräumen. Die Veränderungen des Lichts, die atmosphärischen Effekte und das wechselnde Wetter in Denver stellten eine große Herausforderung an die Architekten bei der Errichtung dieses Gebäudes dar, dessen Fassade sich je nach Lichteinfall und Betrachtungswinkel in ihrer Farbe und ihrem Aussehen ändert.

This building has been conceived as part of a composition of public spaces, museums and accesses to this developing part of town.

L'édifice fait partie d'un ensemble composé d'espaces publics, monuments et accès à cette zone de la ville en constante expansion.

Das Gebäude ist Teil einer Komposition von öffentlichen Räumen, Monumenten und Zugängen in einem Teil der Stadt, der ständig expandiert.

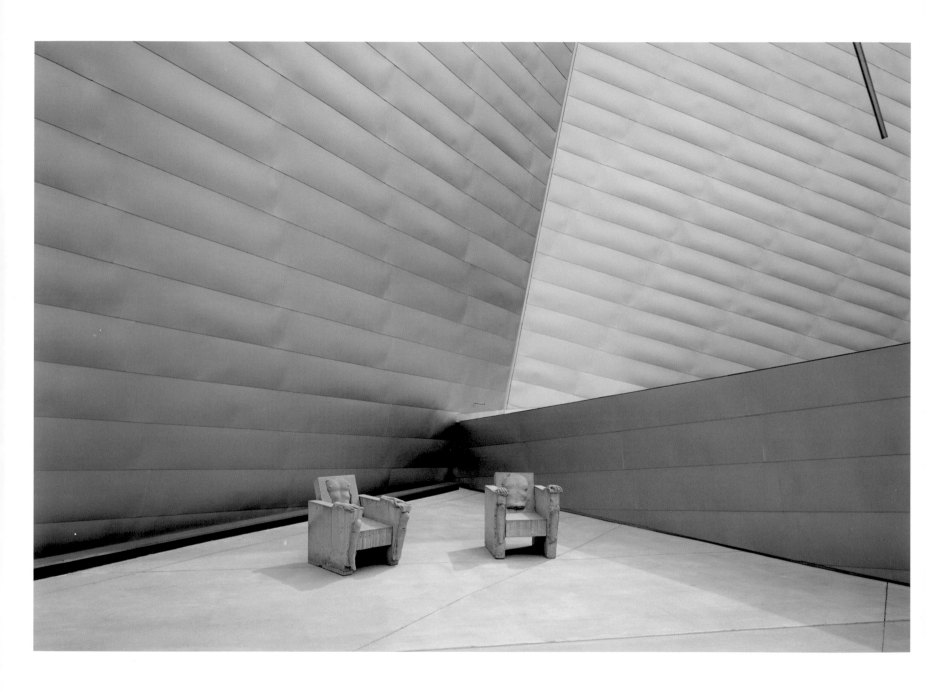

A wide staircase located alongside one of the side walls leads to the exhibition rooms and to a corridor opening onto the performance area.

Un large escalier, inséré dans un des murs latéraux, mène aux galeries d'exposition et à un couloir précédent le théâtre.

Eine breite Treppe an einer der Seitenwände führt zu den Ausstellungsgalerien und zu einem Gang zum Theater.

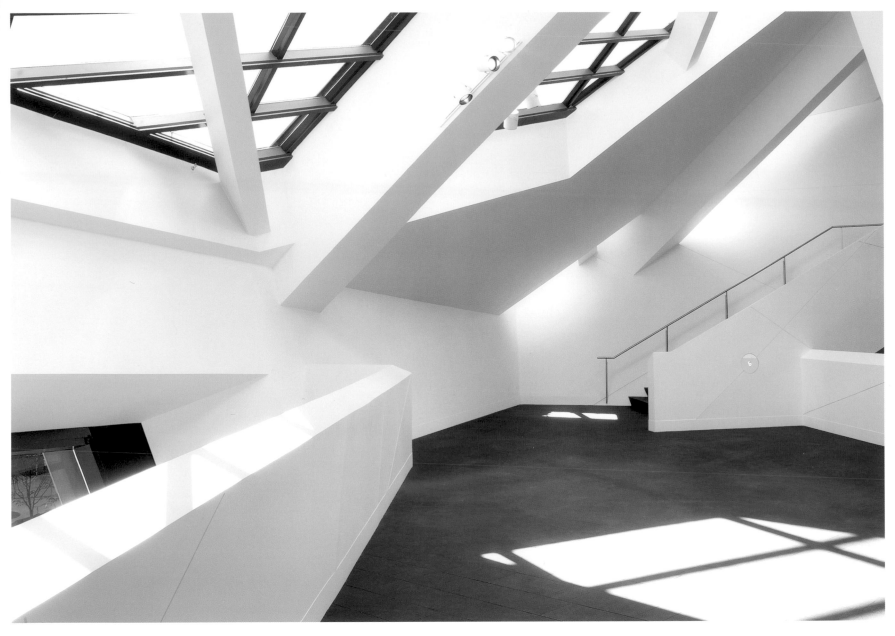

The light, in constant mutation, and Denver's weather conditions constituted the main challenges in the construction of this building.

La lumière, en mutation constante, les effets atmosphériques et les changements climatiques propres à Denver ont été les principaux défis à relever dans la construction de l'édifice.

Die ständigen Wetter- und Klimaänderungen, so typisch für Denver, stellten bei der Errichtung des Gebäudes eine große Herausforderung dar.

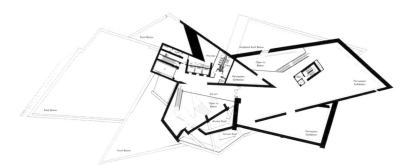

› **Upper level**   Niveau supérieur   Obere Ebene

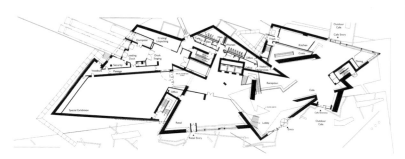

› **Ground floor**   Rez-de-chaussée   Erdgeschoss

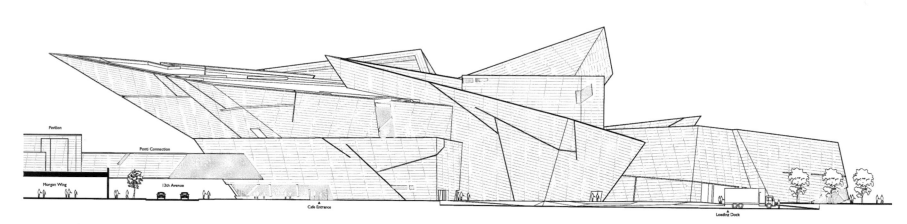

› **Elevation**   Élévation   Aufriss

Selfridges Birmingham

In this case, both the clients and architects set about creating a building that would provide the English city of Birmingham with a modern architectural icon. They situated it in the Bull Ring area, next to a 19th-century neo-Gothic church, so that it would serve as a revitalizing catalyst for the the new urban regeneration of the Digbeth area. The structure is totally curved in all directions and thus shuns any distinction between walls and ceilings; neither does it countenance any right angles to interrupt the continuous, flowing lines, which are based on organic forms. The interior basically consists of a spectacular atrium that receives direct sunlight from an enormous skylight set in the ceiling. The sunshine reflecting against the façade imbues it with colors and visual textures that vary according to the time of day and the atmospheric conditions.

Clients et architectes avaient à cœur de créer un édifice qui deviendrait un icône de l'architecture moderne de Birmingham. Situé dans la zone du Ring Bull, jouxtant une église néogothique du XIXe siècle, il joue le rôle de catalyseur pour dynamiser la récente rénovation urbaine du secteur de Digbeth. Cette structure tout en courbes ne fait aucune différence entre murs et plafonds. Aucun angle droit n'interrompt la fluidité des lignes aux formes fondamentalement organiques. Pour l'essentiel, l'intérieur affiche un atrium spectaculaire inondé de lumière naturelle directe par le biais d'une immense lucarne de toit. La lumière du jour qui se reflète dans la façade change de couleurs et de textures, au gré des conditions atmosphériques et au fil des heures d'en-soleillement.

Die Bauherren und die Planer hatten es sich zum Ziel gesetzt, ein Gebäude zu schaffen, das zu einer modernen Architekturikone in der englischen Stadt Birmingham werden sollte. Als Standort wählte man den Ring Bull, ganz in der Nähe einer neogotischen Kirche aus dem 19. Jahrhundert. Dieses Gebäude verleiht dem Stadtteil Digbeth wieder mehr Leben und Dynamik. Die Struktur krümmt sich in alle Richtungen, so dass sich Wände und Dächer nicht voneinander unterscheiden. Die durchgehenden und fließenden Linien werden nirgendwo von rechten Winkeln unterbrochen; alle Formen sind organisch. Im Inneren wird das Gebäude von einem majestätischen Atrium beherrscht, in das direktes Sonnenlicht durch ein riesiges Dachfenster einfällt. Das Licht, das sich auf der Fassade widerspiegelt, ändert je nach Wetterlage und Tageszeit seine Farbe und visuelle Textur.

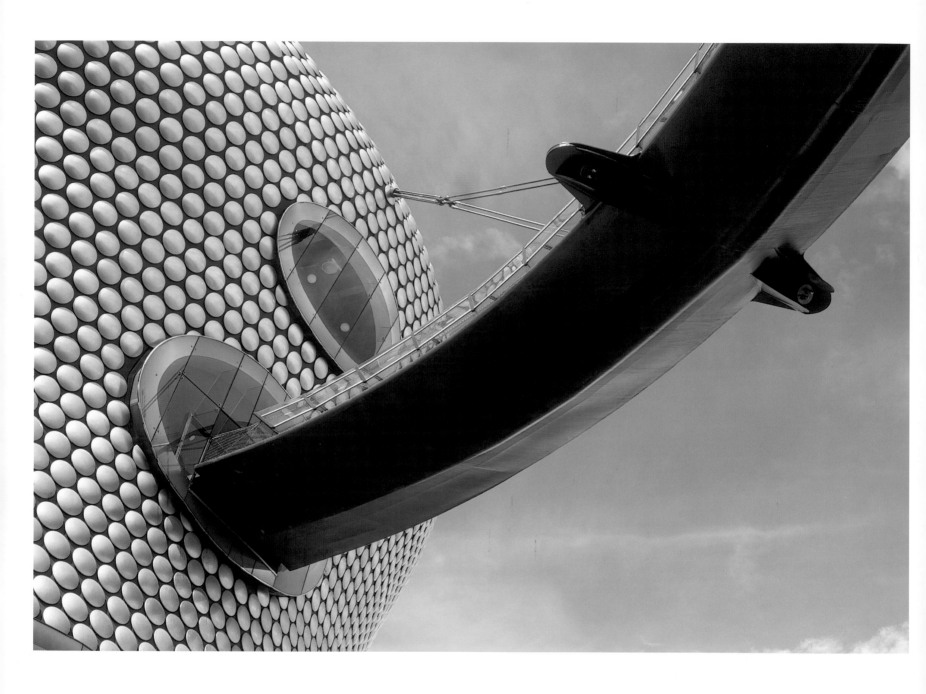

› Location plan Plan de situation Umgebungsplan

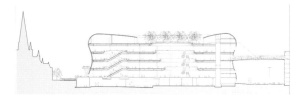

› Section Section Schnitt

Castellum

The theater is the key-stone of a larger development of the new city center. The main focus of this 'Stadshart' is a central square, along the river Rhine. Inevitably, one of the prime ambitions of the theater is to define this public space. The expression of a 'house of culture' needs to be conciliated with the informal character of the square, with shops, bars and restaurants. The building contains a main auditorium seating 749 people, a multi-purpose auditorium seating 240 people, and a movie theater with 3 showing rooms. Since the program was apparently too large for the site, the design was like solving a Japanese puzzle. The main audience and foyers are expressed as one volume, integrating the stage flight. This volume is cladded with an innovative, corrugated aluminium sheet, called desert-storm.

Le théâtre est la clé de voûte d'un vaste programme de développement du nouveau centre de la ville. L'élément phare de ce « Stadshart » est une place, située le long du Rhin. Il est donc évident qu'une des premières missions de ce projet de théâtre soit de définir cet espace public. En effet, la concrétisation d'une « Maison de la culture » doit être en harmonie avec l'aspect informel de la place, avec ses boutiques, bars et restaurants. L'édifice est composé d'un grand auditorium de 749 places, d'une salle polyvalente de 240 sièges et d'un cinéma avec 3 salles. L'envergure du programme dépassant les capacités spatiales du site, le design s'affiche comme la solution à un puzzle japonais. L'auditorium principal + les foyers forment un volume qui intègre la scène. Ce volume est habillé d'une feuille d'aluminium ondulée innovante, appelée tempête de sable.

Das Theater stellt den Grundstein für die weitere Entwicklung eines neuen Zentrums in der Stadt dar. Der Mittelpunkt dieses „Stadshart" ist ein zentraler Platz am Rhein. Und das wichtigste Anliegen der Architekten dieses Theaters war es, diesen öffentlichen Raum zu definieren. Der Ausdruck „Kulturhaus" musste mit dem formfreien Charakter des anliegenden Platzes und seinen Läden, Kneipen und Restaurants vereint werden. In dem Gebäude befindet sich ein Hauptsaal für 749 Zuschauer, ein Vielzwecksaal für 240 Personen und ein Kino mit drei Vorführräumen. Da man all dies nur schwer in dem Gebäude unterbringen konnte, mussten die Architekten am Design lange puzzeln. Der Hauptsaal und die Foyers zeigen sich als ein einziger Körper, der auch die Bühnentreppe mit einschließt. Dieser Körper ist mit innovativen, gewellten Aluminiumplatten verkleidet, die als "Wüstensturm" (desert storm) bezeichnet werden.

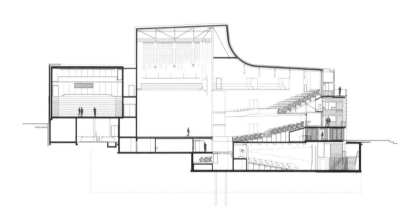

› Section   Section   Schnitt

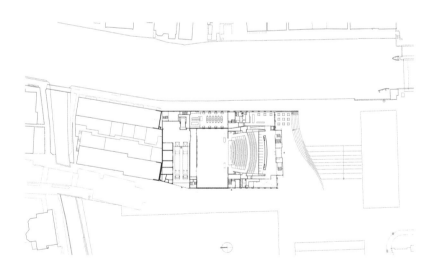

› Location plan   Plan de situation   Umgebungsplan

The theater is the key-stone of a larger development of the new city center.

Le théâtre est la clé de voûte d'un vaste programme de développement du nouveau centre de la ville.

Das Theater stellt den Grundstein für die weitere Entwicklung eines neuen Zentrums in der Stadt dar.

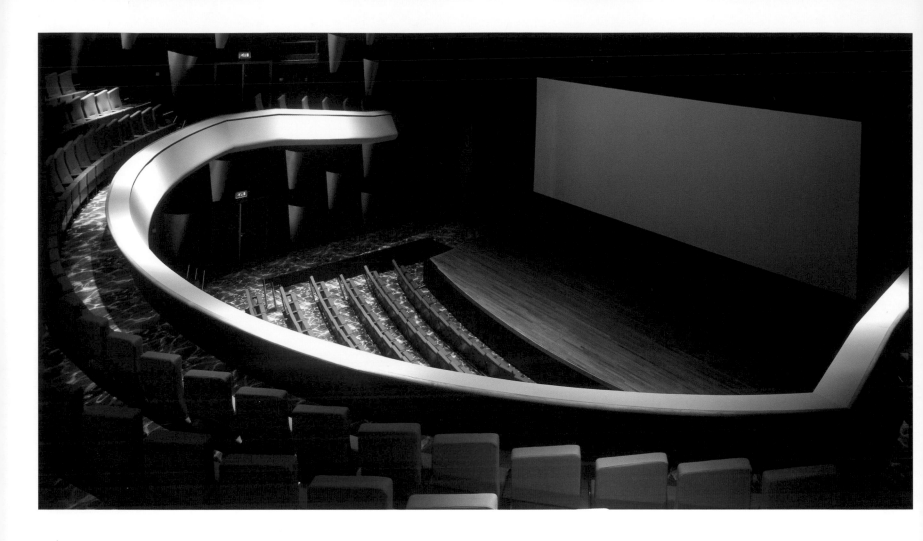

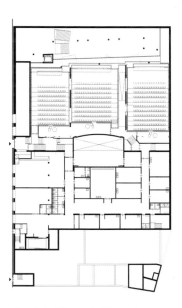

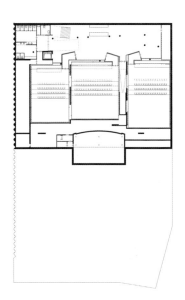

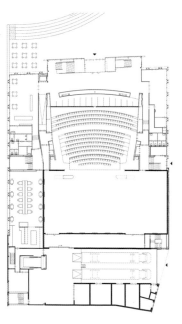

› Level -1 Niveau -1 Ebene -1

› Level -2 Niveau -2 Ebene -2

› Ground floor Rez-de-chaussée Erdgeschoss

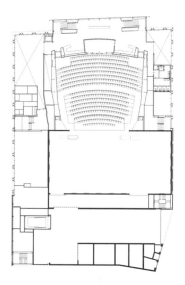

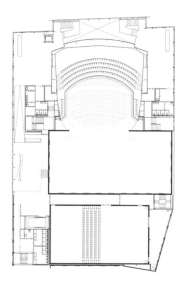

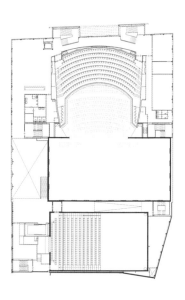

› First floor Premier étage Erstes Obergeschoss

› Second floor Deuxième étage Zweites Obergeschoss

› Third floor Troisième étage Drittens Obergeschoss

Mercedes-Benz Museum
Musée de Mercedes-Benz
Mercedes-Benz Museum

The new Mercedes-Benz Museum, situated at the entrance to Stuttgart, spans 570,000 sq. ft of urbanized space devoted to 120 years of the history of the automobile, via a collection comprising 160 cars and 1,500 unique pieces. The main building seeks to unite tradition and modernity by, on the one hand, displaying the history of the motor company and, on the other, using a futuristic design. State-of-the-art software made it possible to establish controls that assessed the effects of the extremely complicated geometry on all aspects of the building. The exterior façade is made up of steel sheets, as well as large windows comprised of 1,800 separate triangular panes, which make it possible to take advantage of natural light and make great savings in energy.

Situé à l'entrée de la ville, le nouveau Mercedes-Benz Museum abrite 53.000 m² d'espace urbain pour exhiber 120 ans d'histoire de la voiture de collection, avec 160 modèles et 1.500 pièces uniques. L'édifice principal, construction alliant tradition et modernité, expose, d'un côté, l'histoire de l'automobile et de l'autre l'aspect du design futuriste. Cet ensemble est conçu grâce à des ordinateurs de la dernière génération permettant de contrôler les effets d'une géométrie très complexe appliquée à tous les aspects de la construction. La façade extérieure, constituée de lames d'acier, affiche d'immenses baies vitrées formées de 1.800 vitres triangulaires différentes, permettant de bénéficier de la lumière du jour et d'un gain d'énergie considérable.

An der Zufahrt zur Stadt liegt das neue, 53.000 m² große Mercedes-Benz Museum, in dem 120 Jahre der Geschichte des Automobils in Form von 160 Automobilen und 1.500 Einzelstücken gezeigt werden. Im Hauptgebäude treffen Tradition und Modernität aufeinander. Hier wird in einer futuristischen Umgebung die Geschichte dieser Automobilmarke dargestellt. Beim Entwurf wurden Computer der letzten Generation eingesetzt, um die Wirkung dieser komplizierten Geometrie in allen Teilen des Gebäudes festzustellen. Die Außenfassade ist mit Stahlplatten verkleidet und besitzt große Fensterflächen, die aus 1.800 verschiedenen, dreieckigen Gläsern bestehen. So wird das Tageslicht optimal ausgenutzt und sehr viel Energie gespart.

The dual ramp connecting the nine floors of the building around a central atrium is a stunning technical achievement.

Le double itinéraire qui parcourt les neuf étages, véritable prouesse technique, est formé par des rampes descendantes qui entourent un atrium central.

Der zentrale Innenhof ist von Rampen umgeben, die an den neun Stockwerken entlang führen. Technisch aufwendig und für sportliche Menschen.

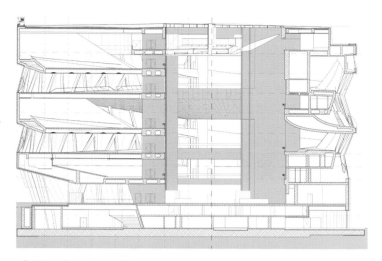

› **Section** Section Schnitt

Prada Aoyama Epicenter

The shape of the building is substantially influenced by the angle of incidence of the local profile. Depending on where the viewer is standing, the body of the building will look more like a crystal or like an archaic type of building with a saddle roof. The ambivalent, always changing, and oscillating character of the building's identity is heightened by the sculptural effect of its glazed surface structure. The rhomboid-shaped grid on the façade is clad on all sides with a combination of convex, concave or flat panels of glass. These differing geometries generate faceted reflections, which enable viewers, both inside and outside the building, to see constantly changing pictures and almost cinematographic perspectives of Prada products, the city and themselves. The fittings with lamps and furniture for the presentation of Prada products and for visitors have been designed especially for this location.

La forme de l'édifice est fortement influencée par l'angle d'incidence du profil local. Selon le point de vue de l'observateur, le corps de l'édifice ressemble davantage à un solitaire ou à un type archaïque de construction avec un toit de tour. Le caractère ambivalent de l'identité de l'édifice, en perpétuel changement, est accentué par l'apparence sculpturale de la structure en verre. La trame rhomboïde de la façade est habillée en alternance de panneaux de verre concaves, convexes ou plats. Ces différentes formes géométriques engendrent des réflexions de facettes qui renvoient aux visiteurs, à l'intérieur comme à l'extérieur de l'édifice, des images modifiées en permanence et des perspectives quasi cinématographiques des produits Prada, de la ville et d'eux-mêmes.

Die Gestalt des Baukörpers ist wesentlich von den Einfallswinkeln des örtlichen Umgebungsprofils beeinflusst: Je nach Standpunkt des Betrachters gleicht der Baukörper eher einem Kristall oder einem archaischen Haustyp mit Satteldach. Diese ambivalente, sich stets verändernde und schwankende Gestaltsidentität des Baukörpers wird noch verstärkt durch die plastische Durchformung seiner gläsernen Oberflächenstruktur. Das rhombenförmige Fassadengitter ist allseitig verkleidet mit konvexen, konkaven oder planen Glasplatten. Diese unterschiedliche geometrische Ausformung der Glasplatten bewirkt facettenartige Spiegelungen, welche dem Betrachter innerhalb und außerhalb des Gebäudes ständig wechselnde Bilder und beinahe kinematographische Sichtwinkel auf die Pradaprodukte, die Stadt und sich selbst ermöglichen. Die Ausstattung des Gebäudes mit Lampen und Möbeln für die Präsentation der Pradaprodukte und für die Besucher wurde neu und speziell für diesen Ort entwickelt.

The glass walls are not made up of the conventional transparent curtain wall, but rather of a structural transparent shell.

Les parois de verre ne se présentent pas sous forme du traditionnel mur rideau transparent, mais d'une enveloppe à la structure transparente.

Die Glaswände bilden nicht die traditionelle, transparente Glasabsperrung, sondern eine transparente, strukturelle Abdeckung.

Thanks to the glass structure, the exterior and the interior merge into a single architectural scenery of creativity and motion.

Grâce à la structure vitrée, l'extérieur et l'intérieur se fondent en un unique paysage architectonique empreint de créativité et de mouvement.

Aufgrund der verglasten Struktur verschmelzen außen und innen zu einer architektonischen Landschaft, die durch Kreativität und Bewegung geprägt wird.

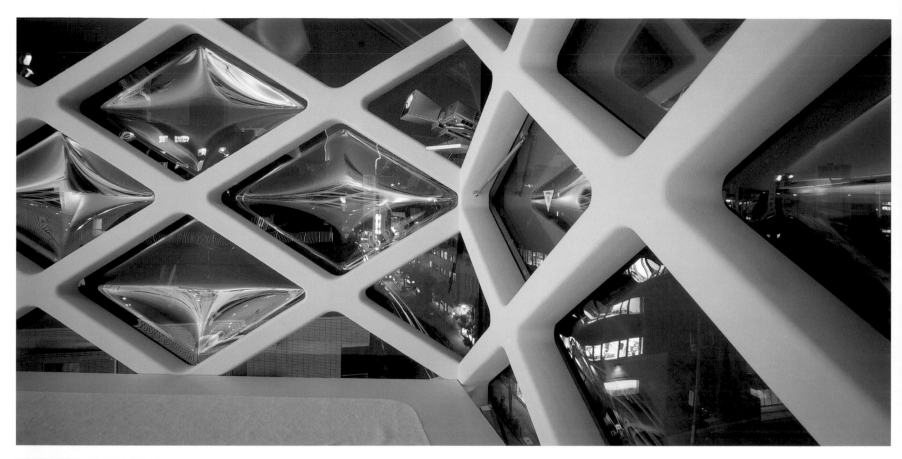

Mahler 4 Tower

The concept of this project sought to break with traditional forms of urban design composition and to achieve a rich urban environment, creating a natural seamless integration with the historic city. The transformation of these ideas is based on two strategies: one is to create a basic three-dimensional structure of interstitial spaces that defines, by subtraction, the volumes of physical development. The other is to avoid the typical formal structure of traditional high-rise building design, and replace it with distinct multi-layered architectural orders. Fulfilling these conditions, the architects transformed the building into three components and reinterpreted the horizontal data of the project into a more dynamic geometry, which results in the exterior fire escape that wraps around the building. The development of the open stair offers additional exterior spaces that can be used as gardens and outdoor extensions at each level.

Le concept, derrière ce projet, vise d'emblée à rompre les modèles traditionnels de design urbain, le transformant en une riche enclave urbaine qui fusionne naturellement avec le centre historique. La concrétisation de ces idées se base sur deux stratégies : créer, d'abord, une structure tridimensionnelle simple, aux espaces intermédiaires, définissant, par extraction, les volumes du développement physique de l'édifice. Il s'agit, ensuite, d'éviter la structure formelle classique du design des édifices élevés, en instaurant un ordre architectonique distinct caractérisé par la multiplicité des niveaux. Forts de ces idées, les architectes ont transformé l'édifice en trois composantes, réinterprétant les formes horizontales du projet par une géométrie plus dynamique qui dérive vers l'escalier d'incendie entourant l'édifice. La construction de cet escalier extérieur crée des espaces qui fonctionnent soit comme des jardins soit comme addenda extérieurs à chaque niveau.

Dieses Gebäudekonzept folgt nicht den traditionellen Modellen, sondern schafft eine wertvolle, andersartige Enklave in der Stadt, die sich auf natürliche Weise an die Altstadt anpasst. Diese Idee setzte man mit Hilfe zweier Strategien um. Zunächst schufen die Architekten eine einfache, dreidimensionale Struktur mit Zwischenräumen, aus denen sich die Gebäudeteile physisch entwickeln. Außerdem vermied man die klassische Struktur von Hochhäusern und führte eine andere architektonische Ordnung ein; gekennzeichnet von vielen veschiedenen Ebenen. Dazu schufen die Planer ein Gebäude mit drei Komponenten, interpretierten die waagerechten Formen neu und ließen eine dynamischere Geometrie entstehen, die der Feuertreppe entspringt, die das Gebäude umgibt. Durch die Konstruktion dieser Treppe entstanden Außenräume, die die Funktion von Gärten erfüllen und äußere Erweiterungen an jede Ebene darstellen.

The development of this open flight of steps offers additional exterior spaces that can be used both as gardens and outdoor extensions at each level.

La construction de cet escalier extérieur crée à chaque étage des espaces jouant, selon le cas, le rôle de jardins ou d'addenda extérieurs.

Durch die Konstruktion dieser Treppe entstanden Außenräume, die die Funktion von Gärten erfüllen und äußere Erweiterungen für jede Ebene darstellen.

› Location plan   Plan de situation   Umgebungsplan

ING Head Offices

In this project, the architects wanted to create a new, high-quality building with a layout that would satisfy modern commercial requirements while also displaying traditional architecture typical of a central European country, in combination with contemporary international design. The new construction is situated on a large lot, and its most striking design feature is its façade, which slopes slightly and incorporates bright steel strips, which create changing visual effects, such as reflections and gleams. This range of contrasts and transparencies is also evident in the atriums inside. The profusion of windows in these communal spaces allows direct natural light, making the whole complex seem transparent.

Dans ce projet, les architectes ont voulu créer un nouvel édifice de haute qualité dont la distribution interne répondrait aux exigences de la technique commerciale actuelle, tout en affichant une architecture traditionnelle, caractéristique d'un pays d'Europe centrale, alliée à un design international contemporain. Le nouveau bâtiment, situé sur un grand terrain, offre un design qui se distingue essentiellement par son esthétique externe. La façade légèrement inclinée intègre des bandes en acier brillant, créant des effets visuels changeants, reflets et éclats lumineux. Cette multitude d'effets visuels, contrastes, jeux et transparences se répète dans les atriums intérieurs. Grâce à l'abondance des baies vitrées, ces espaces communs, inondés de lumière du jour directe, se métamorphosent en zones diaphanes, dotant l'ensemble d'une grande transparence.

Innerhalb dieses Bauvorhabens sollte ein neues, qualitativ hochwertiges Gebäude entstehen, dessen innere Aufteilung den Anforderungen des heutigen, kommerziellen Marketings entspricht und das gleichzeitig die typische Architektur dieses zentraleuropäischen Landes zeigt und sie mit internationalem, modernen Design kombiniert. Das neue Gebäude steht auf einem großen Grundstück und hebt sich vor allem durch seine äußere Ästhetik von anderen Bauten ab. Die Fassade ist leicht geneigt und von glänzenden Stahlstreifen bedeckt, die die Umgebung reflektieren und so immer neue visuelle Effekte schaffen. Diese visuellen Veränderungen, Kontraste, Spiele und Transparenzen werden auch in den Vorhallen des Gebäudes fortgesetzt. Durch große Glasflächen fällt viel Tageslicht in die Gemeinschaftsbereiche ein, so dass sie transparent wirken und das gesamte Gebäude durchsichtig zu machen scheinen.

The multiple visual effects and contrasts, the play of lights and transparencies are reflected on the internal atriums.

La multiplicité des effets visuels, contrastes, jeux de lumière et transparences se reflète dans les patios intérieurs.

Die vielfältigen visuellen Effekte, Kontraste, Spiele mit dem Licht und Transparenzen prägen die Vorhallen im Inneren.

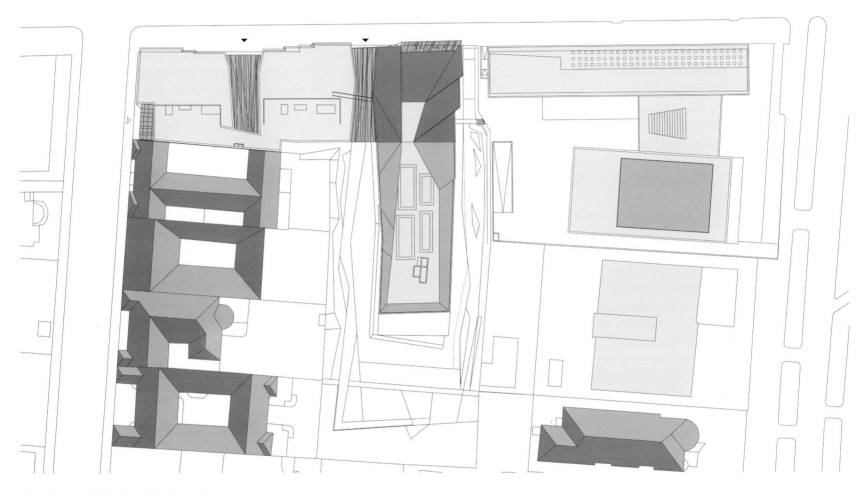

› Location plan   Plan de situation   Umgebungsplan

The hyperkinetic façade of the building contrasts with the traditional robustness of Hungarian architecture, fully integrating with the surroundings thanks to the use of homogeneous materials.

La façade « hyper cinétique » de l'édifice contraste avec la robustesse traditionnelle de l'architecture hongroise, mais s'intègre parfaitement à l'environnement grâce à l'homogénéité de ses matériaux.

Die hyperkinetische Fassade kontrastiert mit der traditionellen Festigkeit der ungarischen Architektur; fügt sich aber dennoch gut in ihre Umgebung ein, weil ähnliche Materialien verwendet wurden.

Norddeutsche Landesbank

The new building occupies an entire city block and is enlivened by extensive greenery, large reflecting pools and public art. The main foyer, exhibition spaces, shops and restaurants are set around a central courtyard, emphasizing the public nature of the place. Energy-saving is the main object of the interior design of the building, which has an open superstructure and windows that provide the ventilation system. 'Double-façade' areas keep out the noise and gas emissions from the heavy traffic and also acts as a duct carrying clean air from the central courtyard to the various offices. Water plays an important part in the design as well, both reflecting daylight and creating a beneficial microclimate. The gardens on the various terraces not only soften the building's appearance, but also encourage a natural form of air-conditioning for its occupants, collecting rainwater for general use inside.

Le nouvel édifice corporatif forme un grand bloc entouré de végétation, d'étangs et de nombreuses oeuvres d'art civil. Dans le vestibule de l'entrée principale, salles d'expositions, boutiques et restaurants, installés autour du patio central, accentuent le caractère public de l'emplacement. L'originalité du design intérieur est le fruit d'une conception orientée vers le gain d'énergie : la superstructure de l'édifice demeure ouverte, les fenêtres assurant le système de ventilation. Les zones de « double façade » le protègent du bruit des rues voisines et des émissions des véhicules, tout en servant de passage pour faire circuler l'air pur du patio central aux bureaux. Les généreux plans d'eau du patio accentuent la réverbération de la lumière du jour et créent un microclimat bénéfique. Sur les terrasses, les grands jardins, outre le fait d'embellir l'édifice, favorisent la climatisation naturelle pour ses occupants, tout en recueillant l'eau de pluie pour l'utilisation générale dans le bâtiment et l'arrosage.

Das neue Firmengebäude nimmt einen ganzen Häuserblock ein und wird durch Vegetation, Teiche und Kunstwerke bereichert. In der Eingangshalle umgeben Ausstellungssäle, Geschäfte und Restaurants einen Innenhof, wodurch sein öffentlicher Charakter verstärkt wird. Bei der Innengestaltung traf man viele Entscheidungen, um Energie zu sparen. So ist die äußere Struktur unbedeckt und die Fenster sorgen für gute Belüftung. Die Bereiche mit „doppelter Fassade" schützen vor dem Lärm der belebten Straßen der Umgebung und vor Autoabgasen. Gleichzeitig sorgen sie dafür, dass die saubere Luft aus dem zentralen Innenhof in den Büroräumen zirkuliert. Große Wasserflächen im Hof spiegeln das Sonnenlicht wider und schaffen ein gesundes Mikroklima. Die großzügigen Gärten auf der Dachterrasse verschönern das Gebäude und klimatisieren es auf natürliche Weise. Sie fangen Regenwasser auf, das für allgemeine Zwecke und zum Gießen benutzt wird.

Übergang West/ Altbau

The interior is characterized by design decisions based on energy efficiency criteria, such as the ventilation system.

L'originalité du design intérieur découle, à l'instar du système de ventilation, des décisions inhérentes à l'usage efficace de sources d'énergie.

Bei der Innengestaltung wurden viele Elemente eingesetzt, um Energie zu sparen, so zum Beispiel das Belüftungssystem.

The array of colors combines with the structure of glass and stainless steel, giving it light and spaciousness.

La multitude de couleurs est en harmonie avec la structure de verre et d'acier inoxydable qui confère à l'édifice lumière et amplitude spatiale.

Die bunten Farben harmonieren mit der Struktur des Glases und Edelstahls und lassen sie hell und weit wirken.

Genzyme Center

The aim of this project was to create offices with a high degree of functionality and flexibility, which provide a sense of corporate identity to the employees, as well as to visitors. From the interior, the building is marked by the interplay of individual elements such as the double façades, openable windows, adjustable sun protection, and colored curtains, all helping to reduce energy loss from the building. An atrium of complex form, with spacious surfaces, open gardens and an openly accessible ground level provide the basis for spatial development. The atrium links together the building's various zones. Stairs between levels create connections and places, leading through gardens which, laid out on terraces, run along the atrium. These are parts of a boulevard which begins in the lobby on the ground level and expanses of water, and with spaces both narrow and broad, composing vistas into the heights.

Le but de ce projet est de créer des bureaux, à la fois hautement fonctionnels et polyvalents, tout en suscitant un sentiment d'identité sociale chez les employés et visiteurs. Vu de l'intérieur, l'édifice se démarque par l'interaction d'une série d'éléments individuels : façades doubles, fenêtres inclinables, protection solaire réglable et rideaux de couleur conçus pour un gain d'énergie efficace. Un atrium aux formes complexes, doté de surfaces amples et de jardins ouverts, formant un accès facile au rez-de-chaussée, base de l'évolution spatiale de l'édifice, relie les différentes zones entre elles. Les petites marches qui relient les différents niveaux créent des liens et des espaces entre les jardins situés sur les terrasses tout autour de l'atrium. Elles font partie d'un boulevard qui part du vestibule au rez-de-chaussée de l'édifice, composé de plans d'eau jouxtant des espaces de différentes tailles, produisant des perspectives différentes de celles créées par les hauteurs de l'édifice.

Die Bauherren wünschten sich funktionelle und vielseitige Büros, die gleichzeitig den Angestellten und Besuchern das Firmenimage übermitteln. Im Inneren findet durch eine Reihe von individuellen, energiesparenden Elementen eine Interaktion statt, z. B. durch doppelte Fassaden, Klappfenster, den regulierbaren Einfall des Tageslichts und farbige Gardinen. Ein Atrium mit komplexen Formen, großen Flächen, offenen Gärten und einer leicht zugänglichen Ebene auf Bodenhöhe, dient als Achse für die Raumaufteilung. Es verbindet die verschiedenen Zonen miteinander. Die Treppen zwischen den verschiedenen Ebenen schaffen Verbindungen und Räume zwischen den Gärten auf den Terrassen an den Seiten des Atriums. Sie gehören zu einem Boulevard, der in der Eingangshalle im Erdgeschoss beginnt, und in der sich verschiedene Wasserflächen und unterschiedlich große Bereiche befinden, durch die das Gebäude in der Höhe unterschiedlich wirkt.

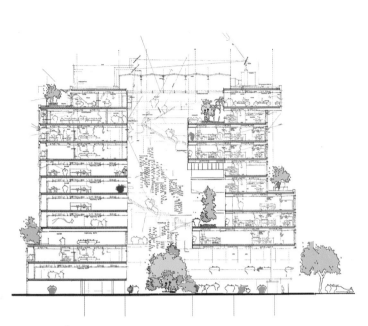

› **Elevation** Élévation Aufriss

› **Plan** Plan Grundriss

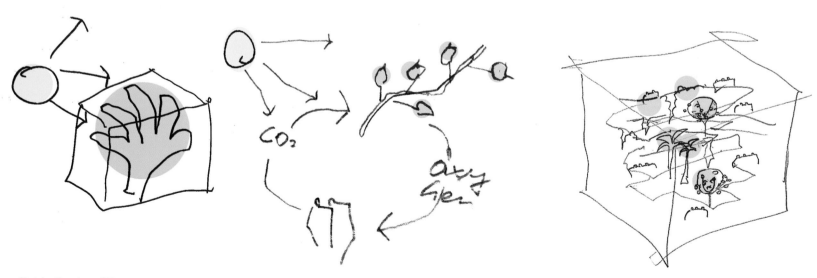

CO_2

› **Sketch** Esquisse Skizze

The object of this project was to create an office block with a high degree of functionality and flexibility.

Ce projet vise à créer des bureaux hautement fonctionnels et flexibles.

Ziel dieses Bauvorhabens war es, sehr funktionelle und vielseitige Büroräume zu schaffen.

TDCCBR Toronto

Situated at the heart of the existing downtown campus, the TDCCBR building creates a new university presence on a busy city thoroughfare. The building is conceived as a 12-story-high transparent rectangular body, elevated above a public concourse, which houses offices, seminar facilities and a faculty cafeteria. The court between the Rosebrugh Building and the TDCCBR creates a large atrium space, whilst single and double-story garden spaces in the upper levels characterize the layout, providing alternative workstations to the individual workspaces. A relatively shallow floor plans enable good use of daylight and allow for natural ventilation. The layering of the façades provides shading and glare protection, and colored elements at balustrade level of the facades contribute towards a distinct individual expression.

Implanté au cœur du campus, l'édifice du TDCCBR forme une nouvelle entité universitaire dans cette ville très fréquentée. Le bâtiment, conçu sous forme de corps rectangulaire transparent de 12 étages, s'élève sur une esplanade et abrite bureaux, salles de cours, et cafétéria des professeurs. Le patio entre l'édifice Rosebrugh et le TDCCBR crée une zone ample en forme d'atrium, face aux jardins à un ou deux niveaux, qui situés aux étages, définissent la distribution de l'espace, tout en offrant des aires de travail, alternatives aux espaces conçus à cet effet. Les sols, relativement plats, permettent d'utiliser facilement la lumière du jour et favorisent la ventilation naturelle de l'édifice. Le revêtement des façades génère de l'ombre et protège de la réverbération du soleil. Les éléments colorés au niveau de la balustrade accentuent son originalité.

Inmitten des Campus liegt das Gebäude der TDCCBR, eine neue Präsenz der Universität in dieser belebten Stadt. Der Bau hat einen transparenten, rechteckigen Körper mit 12 Etagen, der über einem Vorplatz steht und in dem Büros, Unterrichtsräume und die Cafeteria der Fakultät untergebracht sind. Der Innenhof zwischen dem Rosebrugh Gebäude und dem TDCCBR ist eine Art großes Atrium. Die Gärten auf der ersten und zweiten Ebene unterteilen den Raum und schaffen alternative Arbeitsräume. Die relativ flachen Böden tragen zu einer effektiven Nutzung des Sonnenlichts und zur natürlichen Belüftung des Gebäudes bei. Die Verkleidung der Fassaden sorgt für Schatten und schützt vor Sonnenlicht. Durch bunte Elemente am Geländer wird das auffallende Erscheinungsbild des Gebäudes noch unterstrichen.

La Defense

This office complex fits into its urban context as a modest volume with a metal façade that reflects its surroundings like a mirror. As usual in the latest buildings of these Dutch architects, color is the most striking feature. On the exterior walls they have opted for a silvery gray that blends into the urban setting; in contrast, the indoor walls change color in accordance with the time of day, the direction of the sunlight and the position of the observer. The ground plan displays a neutral, rational organization, based on four blocks that form part of two separate volumes of different heights and lengths. These volumes are interconnected (particularly inside) and range from two to five floors in height, according to their function.

Ce bloc de bureaux, inséré dans un environnement urbain, affiche un volume modeste revêtu d'une façade métallique qui, tel un miroir, reflète les alentours. A l'instar des dernières oeuvres des architectes hollandais, la couleur en est l'attrait essentiel : un gris argenté a été sélectionné pour les murs extérieurs en harmonie avec le paysage urbain. En revanche, la surface des murs intérieurs change de couleur en fonction de l'heure de la journée, l'angle d'incidence de la lumière et la place de l'observateur. Le plan s'articule de façon neutre et rationnelle autour de quatre blocs intégrés dans deux volumes séparés, de différentes hauteur et longueur. Ces deux volumes, essentiellement reliés entre eux par l'intérieur, sont de deux à cinq étages, selon la taille et la fonction.

Dieses Bürogebäude fügt sich in die städtische Umgebung als ein bescheidenes Bauwerk mit einer Fassade aus Metall ein, die wie ein Spiegel die Umgebung reflektiert. Der Trend in der modernen holländischen Architektur der letzten Jahre ist, die Farbe in der Ästhetik eines Gebäudes die Hauptrolle spielen zu lassen. In diesem Fall wählte man für die Außenwände ein Silbergrau, das gut zu der umgebenden Stadtlandschaft passt. An den inneren Wänden hingegen ändert sich je nach Tageszeit und Winkel des Lichteinfalls und dem Standort des Betrachters die Farbe der Fläche. Die Raumaufteilung ist neutral und rational. Das Gebäude besteht aus vier Blöcken, die zu zwei getrennten Gebäudeteilen gehören und sich in Höhe und Länge unterscheiden. Diese Gebäudeteile sind im Inneren miteinander verbunden und je nach ihrer Funktion und Größe besitzen sie zwei bis fünf Etagen.

The glass windows of the building exterior are covered with aluminium producing colorful translucent reflections.

Les verrières qui enveloppent la structure extérieure sont habillées d'aluminium et génèrent des reflets translucides aux couleurs brillantes.

Die Fenster an der Fassade sind mit Aluminium verkleidet und wirken wie lichtdurchlässige, glänzende Farbtupfer.

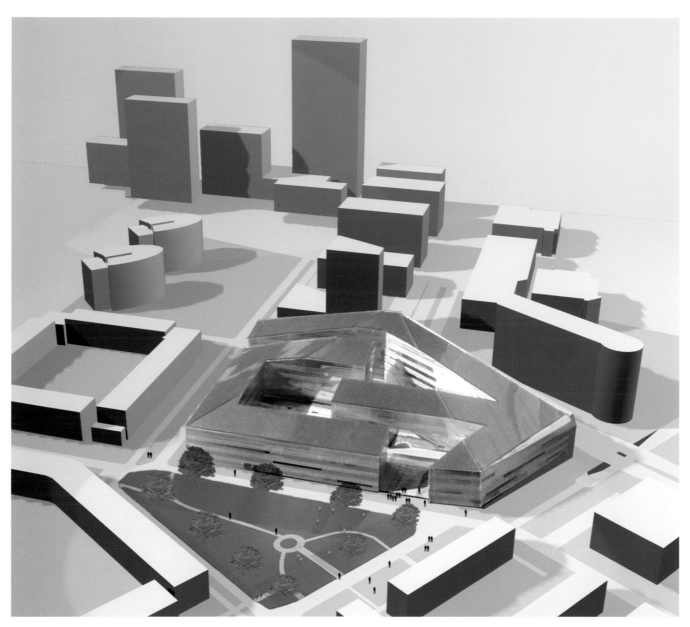

› **Perspective** Perspective Perspektivzeichnung

Dutch embassy Berlin
Ambassade des Pays-Bas à Berlin
Holländische Botschaft Berlin

A continuous trajectory reaching all eight stories of the embassy shapes the building's internal communication. The workspaces are 'carved' out of the main cube and are situated along the façade, while the reception spaces are activated inside the cube. The trajectory works as a main airduct from which fresh air percolates to the offices to be drawn off via the double façade. This ventilation concept is part of a strategy to integrate more functions into one element. Furthermore this integration strategy is also used with the structural concept. The internal walls, adjacent to the trajectory, consist of criss-crossing beams supporting the entire structure of the building and creating open, translucent spaces on the lower levels. The access road between 'cube' and 'residential wall' acts as a courtyard open to one side to allow a panoramic view over the Spree and the park.

La trajectoire fluide qui dessert les huit étages de l'ambassade configure le système de circulation interne de l'édifice. Les espaces de bureaux, implantés le long de la façade, dessinent des avancées qui émergent du cube principal, alors que les salles de réception sont logées à l'intérieur. Cette rampe joue également le rôle de système d'aération pour faire circuler l'air frais qui pénètre à travers la double façade vers les bureaux. Système qui, hormis sa fonction structurelle, fait partie de la stratégie générale qui consiste à intégrer diverses fonctions en un seul élément. Les parois internes, adjacentes à cette rampe, constituent un treillis de poutres entrelacées qui soutiennent la structure de l'édifice. Les espaces des étages inférieurs sont ainsi ouverts et diaphanes. L'accès, entre le « cube » et le « mur » de la résidence, prend la forme d'un grand jardin bénéficiant de vues panoramiques sur la rivière Spree et le parc environnant.

Eine durchgehende Bahn, die die acht Stockwerke der Botschaft einschließt, stellt das interne Kommunikationssystem des Gebäudes dar. Die Büroräume, die entlang der Fassade liegen, entspringen dem würfelförmigen Hauptkörper, und die Empfangsräume liegen im Inneren des Gebäudes. Die erwähnte Bahn dient auch als Belüftungssystem, durch das frische Luft zirkuliert, die durch die doppelte Fassadenwand bis zu den Büros gelangt. Dieses Belüftungssystem erfüllt nicht nur eine strukturelle Funktion, sondern es ist auch Teil der allgemeinen Strategie, mehrere Funktionen mit einem einzigen Element zu erfüllen. Die an diese Bahn anliegenden Innenwände sind ein Geflecht aus gekreuzten Trägern, welche die Gebäudestruktur tragen. Deshalb wirken die unteren Stockwerke offen und transparent. Der Zugang, der zwischen dem „Würfel" und der „Mauer" liegt, dient als weitläufiger Garten mit Panoramablick über die Spree und den umgebenden Park.

The access road acts as a courtyard with panoramic views over the river Spree and its surrounding park.

La rue d'accès à l'édifice revêt l'allure d'un grand jardin doté de vues panoramiques sur la rivière Spree et le parc qui l'entoure.

Die Zugangsstraße wirkt wie ein weitläufiger Garten mit Panoramablick über die Spree und den umgebenden Park.

The internal walls are a structure of load-bearing beams that cross over each other, supporting the glass floors and the structure of the building.

Les murs internes affichent un lattis de poutres entrecroisées qui soutiennent les étages en verre et supportent la structure de l'édifice.

Die Innenwände bestehen aus einem Flechtwerk aus Trägern, die die verglasten Stockwerke und die Gebäudestruktur halten.

Südwestmetall

This office department with clear-cut proportions and reduced forms is built with an open floor plan with no interior divisions, 250 ft long and 60 ft wide. It draws light and color from the surrounding landscape, which is present in many ways, both directly and indirectly, throughout the building. The metal cladding reflects the scenery outside, while light penetrates through the windows covering the façade. This cladding, which is joined to the roof, consists of paper-thin stainless-steel strips 2 inches wide, specially designed and put together by hand following a format recalling the 'weft and warp' of weaving. Natural light pours in along the entire length of the building, through windows that open outward and are directly supported, along with their frames, on a flat surface.

Cet ensemble de bureaux, aux proportions claires et formes réduites, se répartit sur un seul étage dépourvu de cloisons intérieures. Doté d'une extension de 76 m de long et de 18,5 m de large, il tire sa luminosité et ses couleurs directement du paysage environnant, présent partout sous diverses formes, de façon directe ou indirecte. Le revêtement métallique du bâtiment reflète l'extérieur et la lumière se projette vers l'intérieur par le biais de baies vitrées qui couvrent la façade. Ce revêtement est constitué de feuilles d'acier inoxydable de 0,4 mm d'épaisseur et de 5 cm de long, conçues à cet effet et œuvrées à la main, à l'instar d'un treillis en forme de « chaîne et de trame ». La « chaîne » recouvrant l'édifice, reliée au toit, est d'une plus grande précision. La lumière est ainsi visible sur toute la surface longitudinale de l'édifice : les baies vitrées et leurs cadres qui s'appuient directement sur une surface plane, ne peuvent s'ouvrir que de l'extérieur.

Die Geschäftsstelle ist ein eingeschossiger, in seinem Inneren ungeteilter Raum von klarer Proportion und reduzierter Form. Das 76 m lange und 18,5 m breite Haus nimmt Licht und Farben der Umgebung auf und macht sie damit auf vielfältige Weise direkt und indirekt präsent: Während die metallische Rahmung des Gebäudes die Umgebung reflektiert, bricht sich das, durch die Glasfassaden eintretende, Licht an den vier weißen Kuben. Das Metallgeflecht besteht aus nur 0,4 mm dünnen und 5 cm breiten Edelstahlbändern, die in einem speziell entwickelten „Webstuhl" wie „Kette und Schuss" zu Geflechtbahnen verarbeitet wurden. Mit höchster Präzision legt sich die Flechthaut nahtlos um das Gebäude; das Dach eingeschlossen. Auch an der Längsseite ist die Klarheit des gerahmten Kubus zu spüren: Die Fenster und ihre Profile liegen völlig plan in einer Ebene; zum Öffnen werden sie aus der Fensterfront herausgefahren.

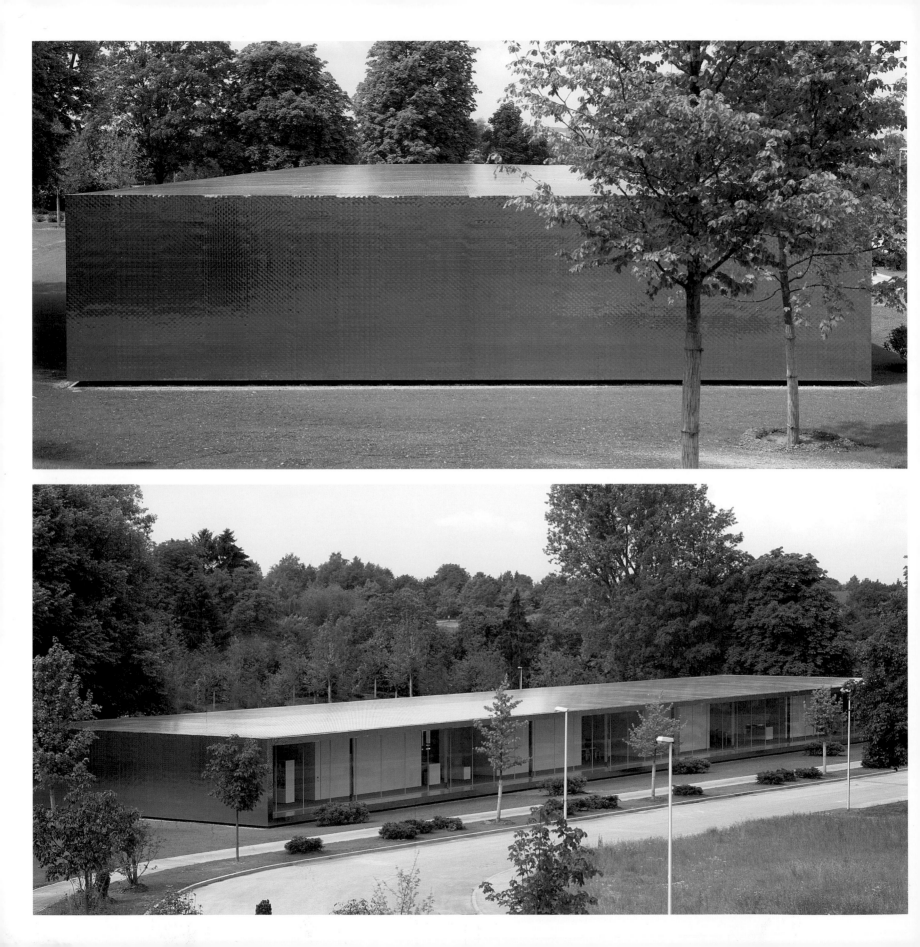

Light and color are taken from the surrounding landscape in many different ways, both directly and indirectly.

De maintes façons, directement ou indirectement, l'édifice puise sa lumière et ses couleurs au coeur de son environnement paysagé.

Die Beleuchtung und Farben des Gebäudes sind direkt und indirekt von der formenreichen, umgebenden Landschaft inspiriert.

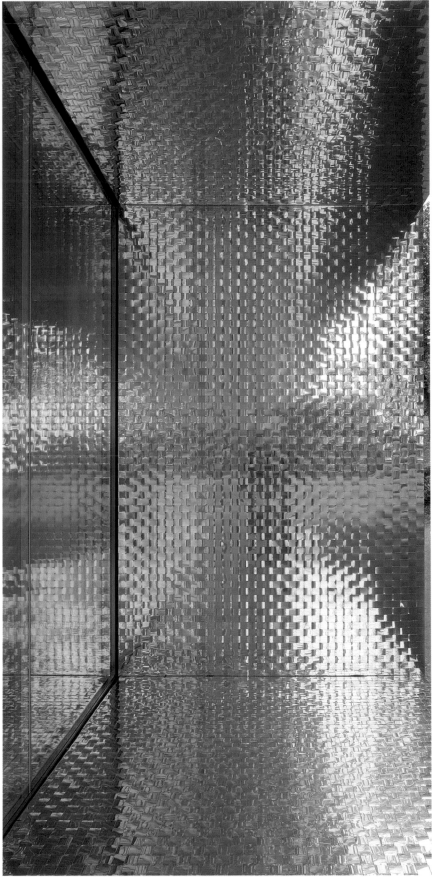

The offices take full advantage of the natural light that comes through the large windows and glass doors.

Les bureaux bénéficient entièrement de la lumière du jour qui pénètre par les grandes baies et portes vitrées.

In den Büros wird überall das Tageslicht ausgenutzt, das durch die großen Glasfenster und Türen strömt.

Berliner Congress Center (BCC)

In the 1960s, the star architect of the former East Germany, Hermann Henselmann, created a visionary complex, the Berliner Congress Center, with a functionality and transparency that gave it a futuristic look. Since 2003, the modernized building has provided over 108,000 sq. ft of surface area for various uses, complete with the latest technology. The BCC stands out on account of its transparency, its strong forms and its numerous complementary architectural details. The building's shiny aluminum dome can be seen from afar and its foyers offer an all-embracing view of the city. Its connection to the Haus des Lehrers results in a unique architectural ensemble around Alexanderplatz.

L'architecte icône de l'ex-Allemagne de l'Est, Hermann Henselmann, influencé par le mouvement Bauhaus, a créé dans les années 60, un ensemble d'édifices à l'architecture visionnaire, le Berliner Congress Center devenu, par sa fonctionnalité et transparence, un style d'architecture futuriste. Depuis 2003, l'édifice modernisé offre 10.000 m² de surface à usages polyvalents, équipés de la plus haute technologie de pointe. Le BCC se distingue pour sa transparence, ses formes claires et les nombreux détails architecturaux qui les agrémentent. De loin, on voit briller la coupole d'aluminium de l'édifice dont les vestibules offrent une vue complète sur la ville. Son lien formel avec sa voisine, la Haus des Lehrers, crée un univers architectural unique autour de l'Alexanderplatz, au cœur même de la cité.

Der vom Bauhaus beeinflusste DDR-Stararchitekt Hermann Henselmann kreierte in den 60er Jahren mit dem Berliner Congress Center einen visionären Gebäudekomplex, bei dem Funktionalität und Transparenz in einer futuristischen Architektur umgesetzt wurden. Das modernisierte Gebäude bietet seit 2003 auf 10.000 m² Fläche hochflexible, und mit der neuesten Technologie ausgestattete, Veranstaltungsflächen. Das BCC besticht durch Transparenz, klare Formen und viele interessante architektonische Details. Weithin sichtbar ist die glänzende Aluminiumkuppel. Aus den Foyers eröffnet sich der freie Blick auf die Stadt. Im formalen Zusammenspiel mit dem benachbarten "Haus des Lehrers" bildet das Gebäude ein spannungsreiches Ensemble am Alexanderplatz in Zentrum der Metropole.

Several architectonic details, such as the spiral staircase, are a fusion of Bauhaus style and contemporary design.

De nombreux détails architecturaux, comme l'escalier en colimaçon, reflètent la fusion entre le style Bauhaus et le design contemporain.

Die zahlreichen architektonischen Einzelheiten, wie die Wendeltreppe, zeigen die Fusion des Bauhaus-Stils mit dem zeitgenössischen Design.

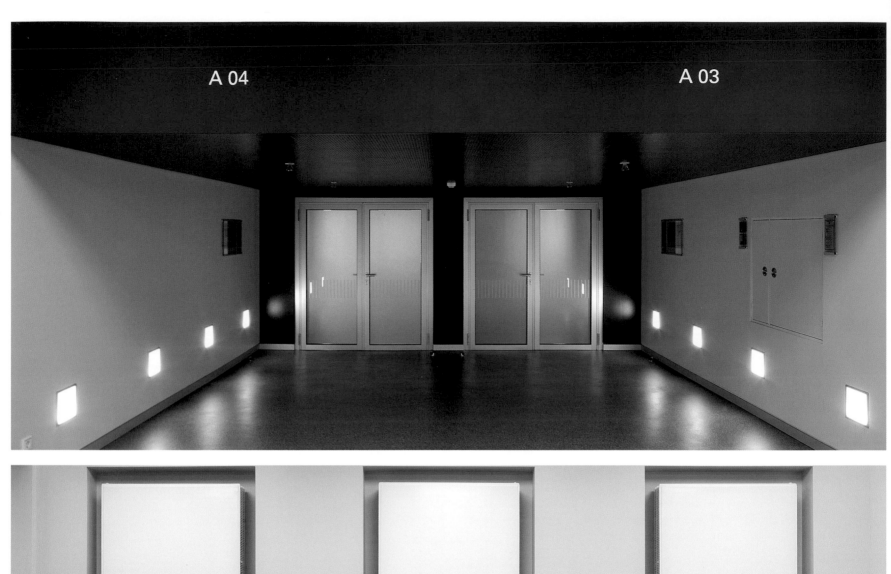

A 04   A 03

Funder Factory 3

The task was to transform a building originally meant as a factory into an exceptional work of architecture. The basic concept involved converting the production area – or production hall – into sculpturally designed elements. Right at the beginning of the design stage, the energy plant, communication gangway, offices, laboratory and access were studied individually with the idea of combining them all into one bold complex, endowed with a body and a head. The reshaping of the energy plant, crowned with 'dancing' chimneys, the use of the gangway as a symbolic link between production and energy, the liberated form of the wing-shaped roof, as well as the sculpted ceilings of the entrance halls and the glass panel gradually disintegrating into the southern-most corner of the building are all elements that break sharply from the central hall, which deliberately remains white and translucent.

Ce projet vise à faire de cet édifice, conçu pour être une usine, une œuvre architecturale exceptionnelle. Le concept de base prévoit de réorganiser la zone de production, ou salle de production, en éléments au design sculptural. Dès le départ, centrale d'énergie, passerelle de communication, bureaux, laboratoire et accès ont été conçus individuellement pour former un ensemble exceptionnel, doté d'un corps et d'une tête. La réalisation sculpturale de la centrale d'énergie, couronnée de ses cheminées dansantes, l'utilisation de la passerelle de circulation comme trait d'union symbolique entre production et énergie, la forme libre du toit, flottante à l'instar d'une aile, ou encore les plafonds sculptés des accès à l'édifice, sans oublier la paroi de verre qui se désintègre graduellement dans l'angle le plus septentrional de l'édifice, sont autant d'éléments qui se distinguent de la salle principale, espace délibérément blanc et diaphane.

Im Rahmen dieses Bauvorhabens wurde eine Fabrik in ein architektonisch wertvolles Gebäude umgestaltet. Dabei setzte man die Idee um, die ehemaligen Produktionsbereiche in skulpturelle Elemente zu verwandeln. Die Energiezentrale, die Verbindungsbrücke, die Büros, das Labor und die Zugänge wurden individuell so behandelt, dass ein Gesamtbild entstand, das das Gebäude einzigartig und unverwechselbar macht. Die plastische Lösung für die Energiezentrale mit ihren tanzenden Schornsteinen, die Verwendung der Verbindungsbrücke als symbolische Verbindung zwischen Produktion und Energie, die freie Form des Daches, das wie ein Flügel über dem Gebäude schwebt, die interessant geformten Dächer über dem Eingang und die Glaswand, die sich an der nördlichen Ecke des Gebäudes langsam aufzulösen scheint; alle diese Elemente sieht man vom Hauptsalon aus, der bewusst als ein weißer und transparenter Raum gestaltet wurde.

The project involved converting a factory building into an exceptional work of architecture.

Le projet vise à transformer un édifice, conçu pour être une usine, en une oeuvre architecturale de valeur.

Im Rahmen dieses Bauvorhabens wurde eine Fabrik in ein architektonisch interessantes Gebäude umgestaltet.

The Boston Convention & Exhibition Center

This project involves a 1.7 million-square-foot convention facility. The long, metallic, double-curved roof of the center soars out to the north and slopes gradually from the 200-foot-tall business district down to the 40-foot-tall residential neighborhoods at the southern boundary of the site. Symmetrically located to either side of the main roof are the lower roofs, covering each side of the exhibit halls. The gradual slope of the main roof along with the lower articulated building massing on the sides mitigate the great size of the exhibit halls and the disparity in scale with the surrounding environment typical of this kind of building. The entire complex is surrounded by a one-way ring road accessible from the back of the building, allowing visitors to come in through any of the four lobbies leading to the individual conference rooms and exhibition halls.

Ce projet comprend la construction d'un centre de congrès de 155.000 m². La toiture de l'édifice, allongée, métallique et doublement incurvée, s'élance vers le Nord, s'inclinant depuis le quartier commercial à une hauteur de 60,96 m vers les zones résidentielles de trois étages, pour descendre de 12,19 m de haut à l'extrémité septentrionale de l'emplacement. Les toitures inférieures se situent de chaque côté de la toiture principale. Chacune d'elles abrite une des salles d'exposition. La pente progressive de la toiture principale et l'édifice latéral moins élevé sur les côtés relativisent la sensation d'immensité spatiale des salles d'expositions, ainsi que le contraste dimensionnel par rapport à l'environnement, caractéristique de ce genre de bâtiment. Le complexe est ceint dans sa totalité d'une route circulaire à laquelle on accède par l'arrière de l'édifice et qui permet aux visiteurs d'atteindre n'importe quel des quatre vestibules latéraux, situés à l'entrée de chacune des salles de réunions et d'expositions.

Innerhalb dieses Bauvorhabens wurde ein 155.000 m² großes Kongresszentrum errichtet. Das lange Gebäudedach aus Metall ist doppelt gekrümmt. Es erhebt sich nach Norden und neigt sich von dem 60,96 m hohen Handelsdistrikt zu den dreistöckigen, 12,19 m hohen Wohngebieten am nördlichen Ende des Grundstücks. Auf beiden Seiten des Hauptdaches befinden sich kleinere Dächer, die die Ausstellungssäle decken. Die allmähliche Neigung des Hauptdaches, das seitliche Gebäude und die geringere Höhe an den Seiten lassen die großen Ausstellungssäle kleiner wirken und verringern den Kontrast zwischen der Größe des Gebäudes und der Umgebung, der so typisch für diese Art von Bauten ist. Der Gebäudekomplex ist von einer Ringstraße umgeben, die man vom hinteren Teil des Gebäudes aus erreicht. So haben die Besucher von jeder der vier seitlichen Eingangshallen, die es vor allen Ausstellungs- und Kongresssälen gibt, Zutritt.

The long, metallic, double-curved roof is the great protagonist of this project.

La toiture de l'édifice, longue, métallique et doublement incurvée, est l'élément phare de ce projet.

Das lange, doppelt gekrümmte Gebäudedach aus Metall ist der Blickfang dieses Gebäudes.

› Elevation Élévation Aufriss

Madrid-Barajas Airport
Aéroport de Madrid-Barajas
Madrid-Barajas Flughafen

The new terminal of the Madrid-Barajas international airport was intended as the new gateway to southern Europe, catering to the needs of 67 to 70 million passengers every year. The architectural design embraces various concepts, including functionality, visual attractiveness and interaction with the natural surroundings. The main achievement lies in the materials used and the impeccable deployment of light, based on bamboo parasols and large glass skylights, as well as an exterior roof made up of a double layer of aluminum, resembling the outspread wings of a bird. The complex is organized into six floors or independent metal modules, visually unified by means of outer claddings and rooftop lawns (which make the terminal look like a huge garden from the air).

Le nouveau terminal de l'aéroport international Madrid-Barajas, destiné à être la nouvelle porte du sud de l'Europe, devrait accueillir entre 67 et 70 millions de passagers annuels. Fonctionnalité, esthétique et interaction avec l'environnement naturel, tels sont les concepts réunis dans l'expression architecturale. La grande réussite des architectes repose sur les matériaux employés et l'utilisation idéale de la lumière : brise-soleil de bambou, grandes lucarnes de verre et couverture extérieure composée d'une double chemise d'aluminium, à l'instar des ailes déployées d'un oiseau. L'ensemble s'articule autour de six étages, sous forme de modules métalliques indépendants, réunis visuellement par des revêtements extérieurs et des toitures de gazon. Vu du ciel, il revêt l'apparence d'un immense jardin.

Der neue Terminal des internationalen Flughafens Madrid-Barajas sollte das neue Eingangstor zum Süden Europas werden. Man erwartet dort zwischen 67 und 70 Millionen Fluggäste jährlich. In der Architektur dieses Terminals treffen mehrere Konzepte aufeinander, nämlich die Funktionalität, die Ästhetik und die Interaktion mit der umgebenden Stadt Madrid. Besonders ist die meisterhafte Verwendung der Materialien und des Lichtes zu erwähnen, das durch Bambusmarkisen und große Dachfenster aus Glas dringt. Ebenso interessant ist das Dach, das aus einer doppelten Aluminiumkonstruktion besteht, die den gespannten Flügeln eines Vogels gleicht. Das Gebäude untergliedert sich in sechs Ebenen oder unabhängige Metallmodule, die visuell durch die Außenverkleidung und Grasdächer vereint werden. Diese Aufteilung und Gestaltung lässt den Terminal von oben gesehen wie einen riesigen Garten wirken.

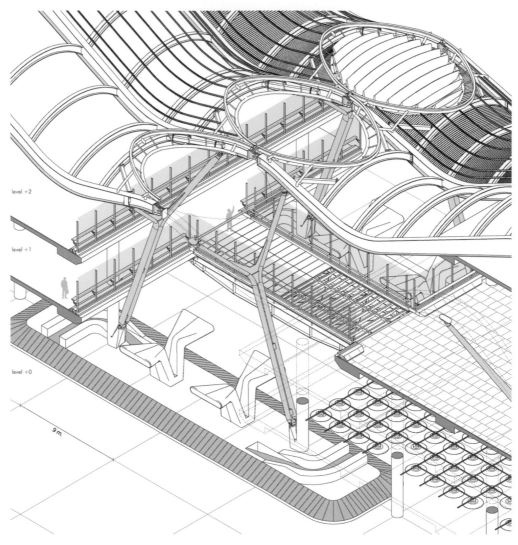

level +2

level +1

level +0

9 m.

> **Axonometry**   Axonométrie   Axonometrische Ansicht

The uniqueness of this airport stands on the building's exposed framework and Y-shaped columns that support the main structural beams.

La particularité de l'aéroport réside dans l'ossature apparente de l'édifice et des piliers en Y qui soutiennent les poutres principales.

Die Y-Form der Träger und des Skeletts, das von den Hauptträgern gehalten wird, machen das Flughafengebäude einmalig.

Natural daylight flows in through large skylights, changing according to the time of day and reflected by the glass surfaces of the bridges.

Les grandes ouvertures du plafond permettent à la lumière d'entrer directement, modifiant ainsi l'aspect de l'édifice au fil des heures du jour, effet accentué par les sols en verre des passerelles.

Durch große Dachfenster fällt viel Licht ein, das das Aussehen des Gebäudes ständig verändert. Die Glasböden der Brücken verstärken diese Wirkung.

› Elevation Élévation Aufriss

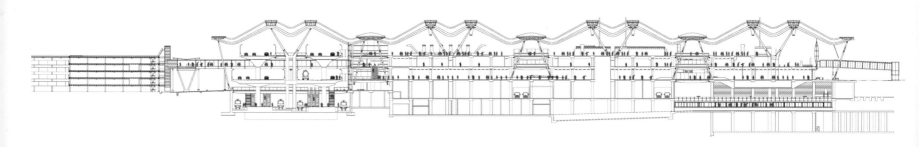

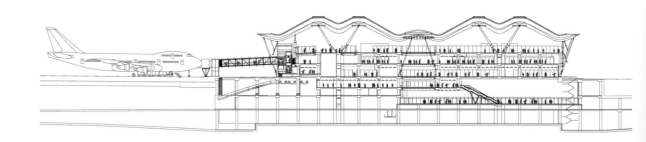

› Sections Sections Schnitte

190

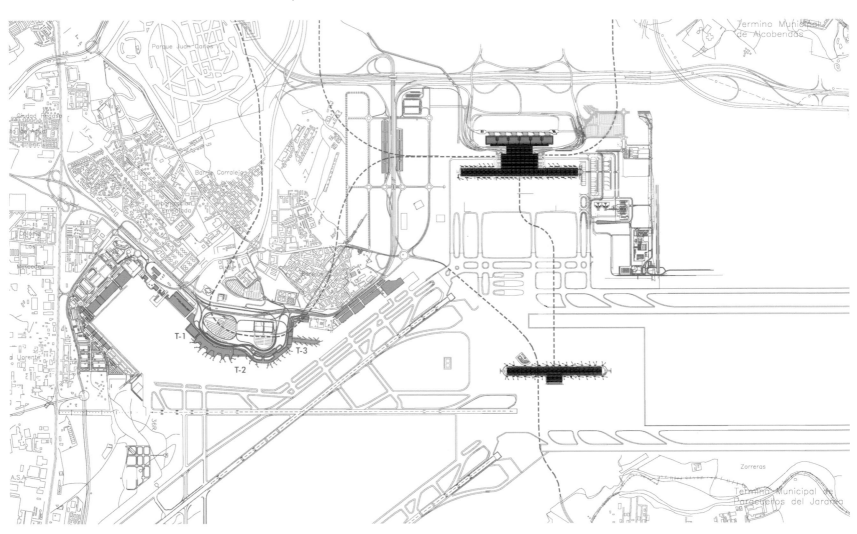

› Location plan   Plan de situation   Umgebungsplan

München Airport Center (MAC)

The MAC creates a visible and livable identity and represents the airport, the city and the region as a modern and technological complex. The shape of the roof, the hall and the portals, as well as the interior space contribute to the special character of the structure. The overall plan consists of open, covered and enclosed spaces, drawing the surrounding landscape into the architecture. This synthesis of built form and varied landscapes presents a rich sequence of forms, spaces and colors. Conceptually, the normal division between interior and exterior space is broken down, a transition is made from high technology to nature. Seen from the road leading to the airport, the MAC roof becomes the visible symbol of the airport. It creates spatial orientation for the passenger terminal area and gives the airport identity and order.

Le MAC crée une identité visible et dynamique qui présente l'aéroport, la région et Munich, comme un ensemble urbain technologique et moderne. La forme du toit, le vestibule, les portails et surtout l'espace intérieur forgent ensemble une structure originale. Le design affiche des espaces ouverts, couverts et fermés qui absorbent le paysage environnant à l'architecture. La synthèse de la structure construite et la variété des paysages déclinent une séquence riche de formes, espaces et couleurs. Sur le plan conceptuel, le clivage traditionnel entre espaces intérieur et extérieur s'efface en passant graduellement de la technologie de pointe à la nature. Depuis la route qui mène à l'aéroport, la toiture du MAC s'affiche en symbole visible de l'ensemble : elle définit l'orientation spatiale du terminal des passagers et confère à la structure aéroportuaire une identité et un agencement ordonné.

Das MAC schafft eine vitale und sichtbare Identität, die den Flughafen, die Region und München als technologische und moderne Standorte repräsentieren. Sowohl die Form des Daches, die Vorhalle, die Portale als auch der Innenraum verleihen dieser Struktur ihren einzigartigen Charakter. Das Gebäude besteht aus offenen Räumen, Dächern und Umzäunungen, die die umgebende Landschaft in die Architektur integrieren. Die Synthese aus der erbauten Struktur und der landschaftlichen Vielfalt zeigt sich als reiche Sequenz aus Formen, Räumen und Farben. Dieses Konzept löst die traditionelle Trennung zwischen Innen- und Außenraum in einen allmählichen Übergang der fortschrittlichen Technologie in die Natur auf. Wenn man das Dach des MAC von der Zufahrtsstraße zum Flughafen aus betrachtet, ist es das sichtbare Symbol für den Flughafen, weil es die räumliche Orientierung des Passagierterminals definiert und dem Flughafen Identität und Ordnung gibt.

Seen from the road leading to the airport, the roof becomes the visible symbol of the building, giving it its own identity and sense of order.

Depuis la route, la toiture de l'aéroport se profile à l'horizon en symbole visible qui lui confère une identité et un ordre intrinsèques.

Der Blick auf das Dach von der Zufahrtstraße ist zu dem sichtbaren Symbol und Identitätsmerkmal des Flughafens geworden.

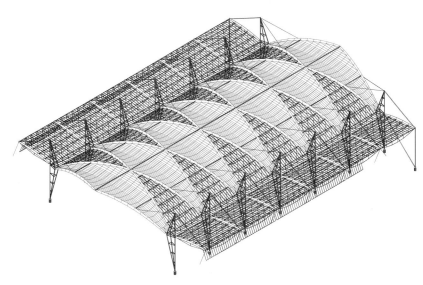

› **Axonometry** Axonométrie Axonometrische Ansicht

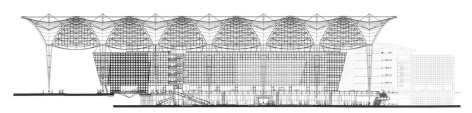

› **Elevation** Élévation Aufriss

Gota de Plata Auditorium

Auditorium Gota de Plata

Gota de Plata Auditorium

This theater, which forms part of a 62-acre cultural park, looms over the middle of a square, combining with it to form a landmark. It establishes a dialogue with the square that is enhanced by the structure of its roof, which stands at a height of 82 ft. The structure acts as a mirror made up of reflecting glass lights, supported by three large steel pillars, and projects 130 ft outward on both sides. In the lower part of the building, an enormous stone podium covering the same area as the roof provides access to the auditorium while also serving as a vantage point for contemplating a mural. The rest of the building is hidden behind a 50-ft-high structure, made up of metal and glass panels, which acts as an anteroom to the venue.

Ce théâtre-auditorium, intégré à un parc culturel de 25 hectares, est situé au coeur d'une place, à l'instar d'un mirador, faisant du binôme théâtre-place le point de mire des visiteurs du parc. Il s'établit ainsi un dialogue, exalté par la structure de la toiture, qui s'élève à 25 m de haut. Celle-ci joue le rôle de miroir composé des scintillements du verre réfléchissant, et qui, reposant sur trois grands piliers d'acier, s'étend de 40 m à chaque extrémité. Dans la partie basse de l'édifice, sous la zone de la toiture, un énorme podium de pierre permet d'accéder au théâtre, tout en formant un mirador du haut duquel on peut observer la peinture murale. Le reste du bâtiment est masqué derrière une structure de 15 m de haut, constituée de panneaux d'acier et de verre, sorte d'antichambre précédant l'enceinte.

Das Theater-Auditorium gehört zu einem 25 Hektar großen Kulturpark und steht mitten auf einem Platz, wo es auch als Aussichtsterrasse dient. Diese Kombination aus Theater und Platz ist der visuelle Anziehungspunkt für die Besucher. So entsteht ein Dialog, der noch durch die Struktur des Daches auf einer Höhe von 25 m verstärkt wird. Diese Struktur dient als eine Art Spiegel, der von den Fenstern aus reflektierendem Glas gebildet wird und die sich auf drei große Stahlsäulen stützt und auf beiden Seiten fast 40 m vorspringt. Im Erdgeschoss des Gebäudes, auf der Fläche unterhalb des Dachbereiches, befindet sich ein riesiges Podium aus Stein, über das man das Theater betritt und das zu einem Aussichtspunkt wird, von dem aus man die Wandmalerei betrachten kann. Der Rest des Gebäudes ist hinter einer 15 m hohen Struktur verborgen, die als Vorhalle zum Schauplatz dient und aus Paneelen aus Glas und Metall besteht.

The construction of the auditorium was completed in only eleven months, using materials such as reinforced and prefabricated concrete, and steel.

Onze mois ont suffi pour construire cet auditorium où se mêlent des matériaux tels le béton armé, le béton préfabriqué et l'acier.

Das Auditorium wurde in nur elf Monaten errichtet. Man kombinierte Materialien wie Stahlbeton, vorgefertigten Beton und Stahl.

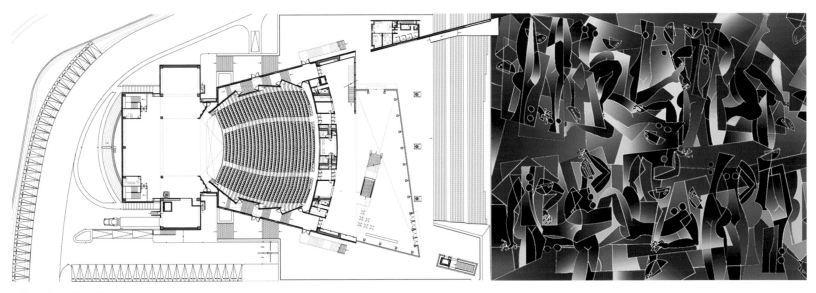

› **Plan** Plan Grundriss

Braga Stadium

Stade de Braga

Braga Stadion

The idea of building a new stadium in the Portuguese city of Braga was sparked by Portugal's nomination as the host of soccer's European Cup in 2004. This stadium turned out to be an exceptional and innovative piece of architecture for various reasons. The main one is the departure from traditional European architectural forms, which dictate that football stadiums are built with an elliptic form. Instead, this stadium was defined by two independent modules situated on either side of the playing pitch, meaning that there are no bleachers or spectators behind the goalposts. Another distinctive feature is the stadium's complete integration into its natural surroundings, to the extent that one side is literally embedded into walls of granite. The other module, in contrast, is open, thereby providing the possibility of enjoying the landscape around the stadium.

L'idée de construire un nouveau stade à Braga, ville portugaise, est le fruit de l'élection du Portugal comme siège de l'organisation de la Coupe d'Europe de Football en 2004. Pour diverses raisons, ce stade est une œuvre d'architecture à la fois exceptionnelle et innovatrice. En effet, cette construction ne suit pas la tradition européenne qui consiste à créer des stades de football en forme d'ellipse. Celui-ci se définit plutôt par des modules autonomes situés des deux côtés du terrain de jeu, de sorte que derrière les cages, il n'y a ni tribune ni public. L'autre aspect essentiel est son insertion totale dans l'environnement naturel, allant jusqu'à situer un de ses côtés littéralement à l'intérieur des murs de granit. En revanche, l'autre module est ouvert, permettant de jouir du paysage environnant l'enceinte.

Als man wusste, dass Portugal Austragungsort für die Fußballeuropameisterschaft 2004 werden sollte, errichtete man in der portugiesischen Stadt Braga ein neues Stadion. Dieses Stadion ist aus verschiedenen Gründen ein außergewöhnliches und innovatives Bauwerk. Hauptsächlich unterscheidet es sich in seiner Form von anderen Sportanlagen, denn es hat nicht die typische, architektonische Form einer Ellipse, wie sie bei europäischen Stadien üblich ist. Die Architekten schufen stattdessen zwei unabhängige Module, die zu beiden Seiten des Spielfeldes liegen. So gibt es hinter den Toren keine Tribünen und keine Zuschauer. Eine andere Besonderheit des Komplexes ist, dass er sich völlig in die Umgebung integriert, und zwar so stark, dass sich eine der Seiten sogar innerhalb der Granitwände befindet. Das Stadion ist offen, so dass man die umgebende Landschaft betrachten kann.

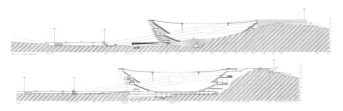

› Sections   Sections   Schnitte

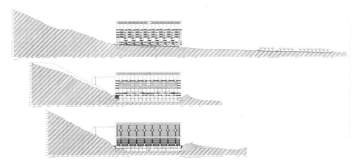

› Elevations   Élévations   Aufrisse

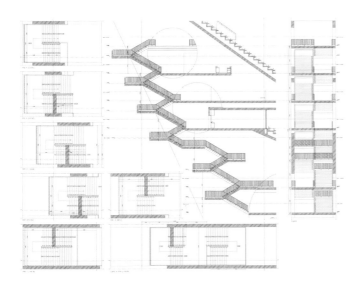

Details of the staircases   Détail d'escalier   Detail des Treppenhauses

The unfinished appearance of this fairground is emphasized by the use of concrete, which is the key protagonist of this construction.

L'aspect volontairement inachevé de l'enceinte est accentué par l'usage du béton, matériau par excellence de la construction.

Das beabsichtigte, unfertige Aussehen des Gebäudes wird durch die Verwendung von Beton als wichtigstes Konstruktionsmaterial noch unterstrichen.

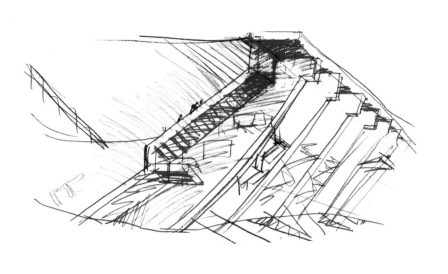

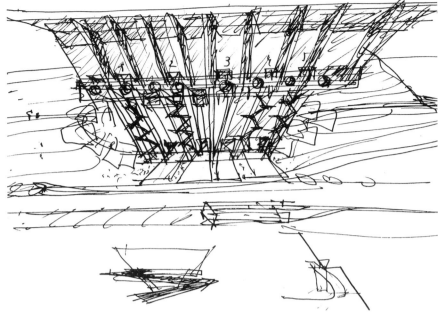

› Sketch   Esquisse   Skizze

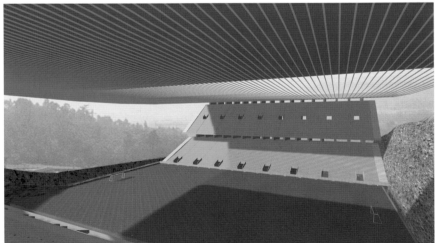

Access to the tribunes is through stairs, elevators and openings that stand out from the stone background located above the stadium.

Situés au-dessus du stade pour assurer l'accès aux tribunes, escaliers, ascenseurs et entrées se détachent sur un fond de pierre.

Man erreicht die Tribünen über Treppen, Aufzüge und Zugänge, die sich vor dem Hintergrund aus Stein erheben und über dem Stadion liegen.

Tenerife Auditorium

Auditorium de Tenerife

Auditorium von Teneriffa

The Tenerife Auditorium has turned the coastal area of Cabo Llanos into the most important leisure zone of the city of Santa Cruz de Tenerife. It is distinguished by the contrast between avant-garde design and the colorfulness typical of the architecture of the Canary Islands. The building's most outstanding elements are the expressive forms of its roofs, characteristic of the work of Santiago Calatrava. One of them, *The Wing*, consists of a large concrete element built as an overhanging triangular floor originating in the rear of the auditorium, supported on the vertex of the central body and stretching up to a height of 190 ft while diminishing in width and thickness. Using the trencadis technique, the white liles make the auditorium stand out from afar, while also reflecting the lights of the city.

L'Auditorium de Tenerife fait de la zone côtière de Cabo Llanos, l'espace de loisir le plus important de la ville de Santa Cruz de Tenerife. Il affiche un contraste entre un design contemporain très avant-gardiste et l'architecture colorée des Iles Canaries. L'édifice est mis en valeur par les formes expressives de ses toitures, caractéristiques de l'architecture de Santiago Calatrava. L'une d'elle, *L'Aile*, est constituée d'une grande pièce en béton formant une surtoiture triangulaire, ancrée à l'arrière de l'auditorium et posée au sommet du noyau central, qui s'élance à 58 m de haut, minimisant ainsi sa largeur et son épaisseur. La finition en trencadís de céramique blanche rend l'auditorium visible de loin et reflète la luminosité de la ville.

Das modern gestaltete Auditorium von Teneriffa lässt einen Kontrast zu der farbigen, typischen Architektur der Kanarischen Inseln entstehen, die es umgibt. So schuf man an diesem Küstenstreifen in Cabo Llanos ein wichtiges Kulturzentrum für die Stadt Santa Cruz de Tenerife. Die auffallendsten Elemente des Gebäudes sind die kraftvollen Formen des Daches; typisch für die Entwürfe des Architekten Santiago Calatrava. Eines dieser Elemente, der so genannte „Flügel", besteht aus einem großen Stück Beton, das ein dreieckiges, überstehendes Dach bildet und am hinteren Teil des Gebäudes angesetzt ist. Dieses Dach stützt sich auf den Scheitel der vorderen Form und erreicht schließlich eine Höhe von 58 Metern. Nach oben wird es schmaler und biegt sich wieder nach unten. Das Gebäude ist mit weißer Keramik in Trencadis-Technik verkleidet. Man kann es schon von weitem leicht erkennen, denn es reflektiert das Licht der Stadt.

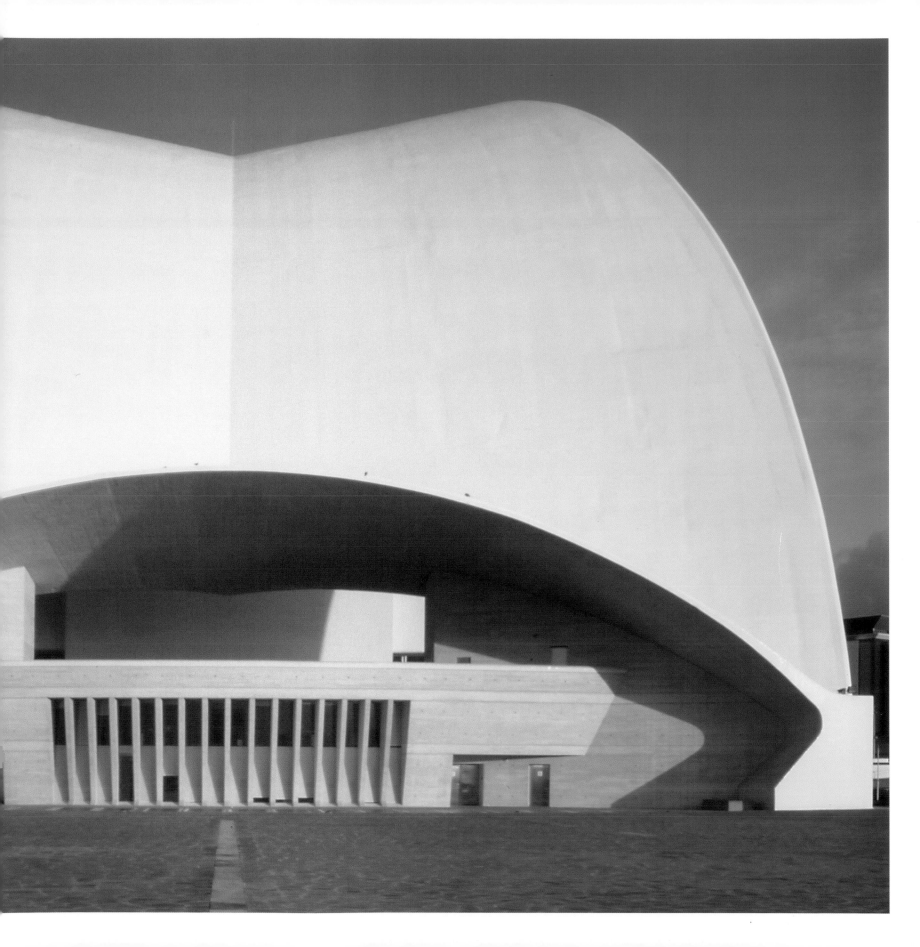

By night the tiled auditorium reflects the city and the sea through visual effects created by the light.

La nuit, les mosaïques de céramique de l'auditorium renvoient l'image de la ville et de la mer en créant un effet visuel composé d'une multitude de plans façonnés par la lumière.

Nachts reflektieren die Mosaiksteinchen die Stadt und das Meer. Dieser visuelle Effekt schafft je nach Lichteinfall verschiedene Ebenen.

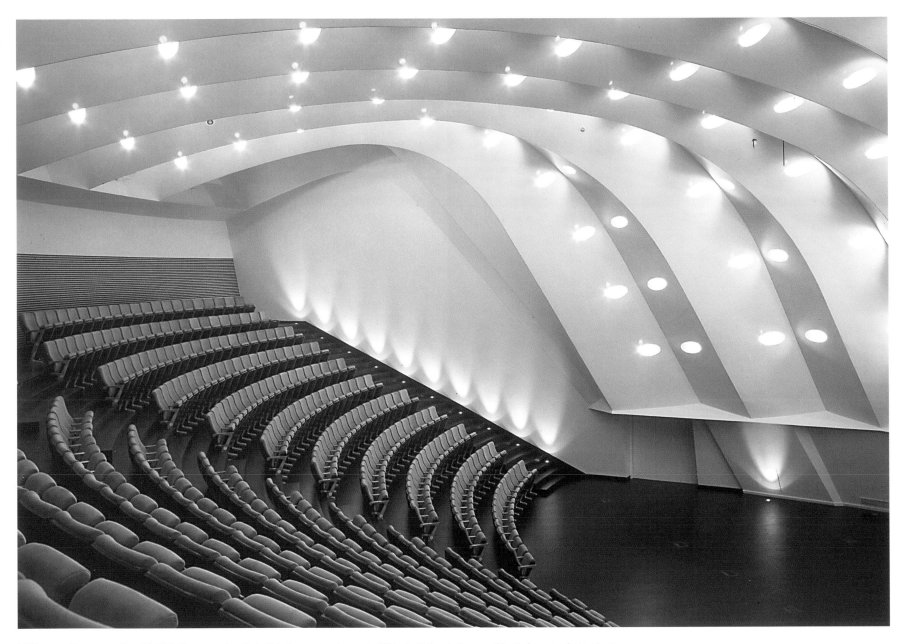

With a seating capacity of 1,600, the symphonic hall is the main element of this building in terms of both form and structure.

La Salle Symphonique, l'élément générateur de l'édifice tant sur le plan formel que structurel, peut accueillir 1.600 personnes.

Der Sinfoniesaal ist das Element, das das Gebäude sowohl formal als auch strukturell bestimmt. Hier finden 1.600 Menschen Platz.

Agbar Tower
Tour Agbar
Agbar Turm

The Agbar Tower has become a reference point for all the inhabitants of Barcelona. The architect Jean Nouvel bore in mind the building's function as the corporate headquarters of a water company to create a small skyscraper that emulates a perfectly constant water spout under stabilized pressure. The main construction materials were concrete, steel and transparent, translucent glass strips. The structure received 4,349 openings, as well as 4,500 windows, and 40 different colors were used. The architectural form consists of two cylinders in the shape of non-concentric ovals, crowned by a dome of steel and glass. The interior cylinder supplies the building's users with means of vertical circulation: service and passenger elevators, staircases and other installations distributed over the various floors.

La tour Agbar est devenue le point de référence de tout Barcelone. L'architecte Jean Nouvel, s'adaptant à son client —le siège social d'une compagnie d'eau— a conçu un petit gratte-ciel qui représente un jet d'eau d'une pression constante, parfaite et stable. Ses matériaux de construction essentiels sont le béton, l'acier et les plaques de verre transparentes et translucides. La structure est dotée de 4.349 ouvertures, d'environ 4.500 fenêtres et de 40 couleurs différentes. L'architecture formelle de l'édifice part de deux cylindres ovales et non concentriques, couronnés d'une coupole de verre et d'acier. Le cylindre intérieur est axé sur la circulation verticale des usagers, par le biais d'escaliers, escalators, ascenseurs et installations réparties sur les différents étages.

Der Agbar Turm ist für die Bewohner Barcelonas bereits zu einem emblematischen Gebäude der Stadt geworden. Der Architekt Jean Nouvel entwarf dieses Gebäude als Sitz des Wasserwerkes. Inspiriert von dem Konzept „Wasser" schuf er einen kleinen Wolkenkratzer, einer Fontäne nachempfunden, die konstant, perfekt und mit gleichem Druck fließt. An dem Gebäude wurden hauptsächlich Beton, Stahl und lichtdurchlässige, transparente Glasplatten verwendet. Die Struktur glänzt in 40 verschiedenen Farben, enthält 4.349 Öffnungen und 4.500 Fenster. Die architektonische Form geht von zwei ovalen, nicht konzentrischen Zylindern aus, die von einer Kuppel aus Glas und Stahl gekrönt werden. Der innere Zylinder dient der vertikalen Bewegung der Benutzer über Treppen, Lastenaufzüge, Aufzüge und Installationen in den verschiedenen Stockwerken.

The modernist architecture of Gaudi and the Montserrat mountains inspired architect Jean Nouvel in the design of the Agbar Tower.

En dessinant la Tour Agbar, l'architecte Jean Nouvel s'est inspiré de l'architecture moderniste de Gaudí et de la montagne catalane de Montserrat.

Die modernistische Architektur Gaudís und die Berge von Montserrat inspirierten den Architekten Jean Nouvel bei der Gestaltung des Turms Agbar.

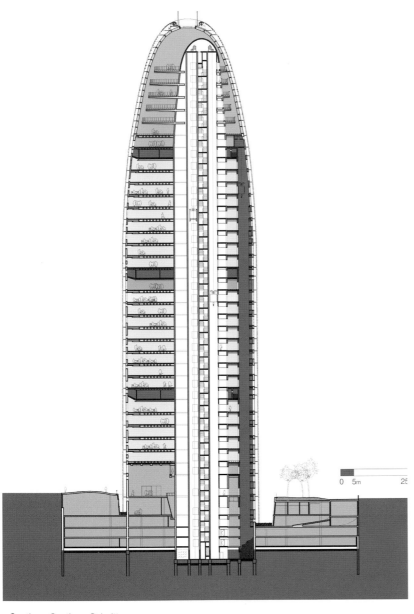

› **Section** Section Schnitt

0 5m 25

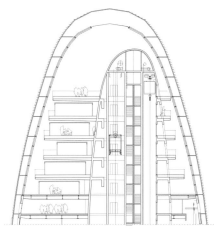

› Section Section Schnitt

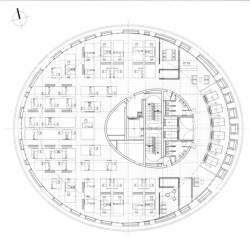

› Plan Plan Grundriss

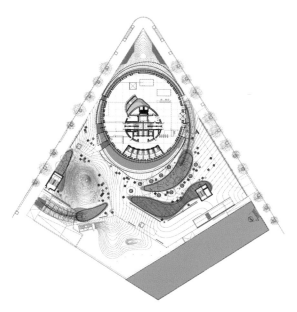

› **Location plan** Plan de situation Umgebungsplan

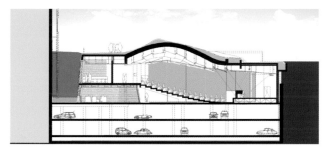

› **Section** Section Schnitt

Following a thorough study of the incidence of sunlight, the glass panels were given varying degrees of transparency in order to soften the colors of the façade.

Les panneaux de verre, aux différents degrés de transparence, adoucissent la façade colorée, grâce à une étude minutieuse de l'incidence de la lumière du jour.

Das Glas ist unterschiedlich stark transparent und lässt die Farben der Fassade verschwimmen. Der Lichteinfall wurde vor dem Einsetzen der Fenster genau analysiert.

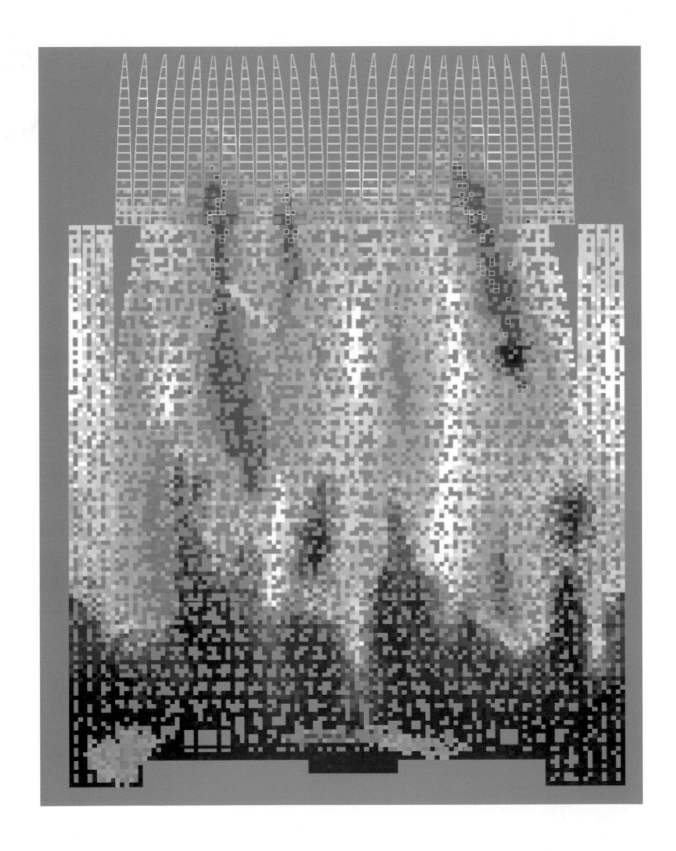

246

Deutsche Post Tower

This office tower belonging to the German postal service is located in the city center, with a height of 533 ft, spread over 41 stories. To build this new skyscraper, the American architects took on the challenges posed by the latest advances in technology, as well as ecological considerations. The tower is an oval, divided along its main axis into two identical halves that are displaced horizontally with respect to each other. These two sections are joined by a 24-ft-wide atrium. The entire façade is covered with glass and this material's flexibility combines with a light, stainless-steel structure to create a highly original, transparent skeleton. This "skin" makes it possible to create shady areas, thanks to the incorporation of a system that filters sunlight.

La tour de bureaux de la poste allemande, située au coeur de la ville, s'élève sur 41 étages, atteignant ainsi 162,5 m de haut. La réalisation de ce gratte-ciel lance un défi aux architectes américains sur les plans de la technologie de pointe et de l'écologie. Cette tour ovale est divisée sur son axe principal en deux parties jumelles, décalées à l'horizontal l'une par rapport à l'autre et reliées entre elles par un atrium de 7,2 m de large. La façade, tout en verre, apporte une souplesse de construction accentuée par une légère structure d'acier inoxydable, façonnant ce squelette transparent au design original. Cette « peau » enveloppant l'édifice permet de créer des zones de clair-obscur, fruits d'un système de filtration des rayons solaires.

Im Zentrum der Stadt Bonn befindet sich in einem 162,5 m hohen Gebäude mit 41 Stockwerken die Hauptverwaltung der Deutschen Post. Die Errichtung dieses neuen Wolkenkratzers war eine Herausforderung für die amerikanischen Architekten, bei der sie hochmoderne Technologie einsetzten und Umweltaspekte berücksichtigten. Das Hochhaus hat eine ovale Form und wird von seiner Hauptachse in zwei gleiche Teile unterteilt, die horizontal ein wenig versetzt liegen. Die beiden Gebäudeteile sind durch einen 7,2 m breites Atrium miteinander verbunden. Die gesamte Fassade besteht aus Glas, ein Material, das in der Architektur sehr vielseitig verwendbar ist. Bei diesem originellen Gebäude wurde es mit einer leichten Edelstahlstruktur kombiniert, die das transparente Skelett bildet. In dieser „Gebäudehaut" konnte man, mit einem Systeme zum Filtern des Lichts, verschiedene helle und dunkle Zonen schaffen.

The key elements of this design are its aerodynamic shape and the use of materials like concrete, steel, and glass.

La forme aérodynamique et l'usage de matériaux de construction, tels le béton, l'acier et le verre sont les éléments clés du design.

Die Hauptgestaltungselemente haben eine aerodynamische Form und sie bestehen aus Konstruktionsmaterialien wie Beton, Stahl und Glas benutzt.

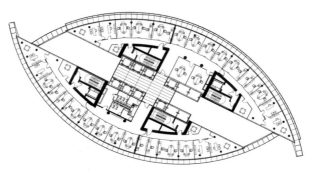

› Plan Plan Grundriss

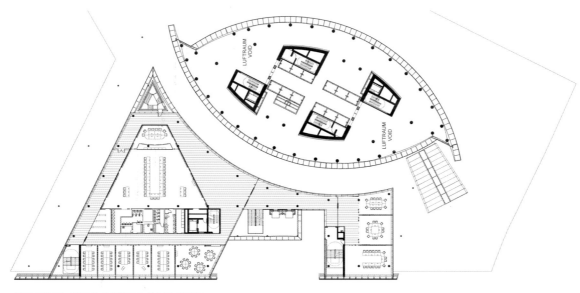

› Upper level Niveau supérieur Obere Ebene

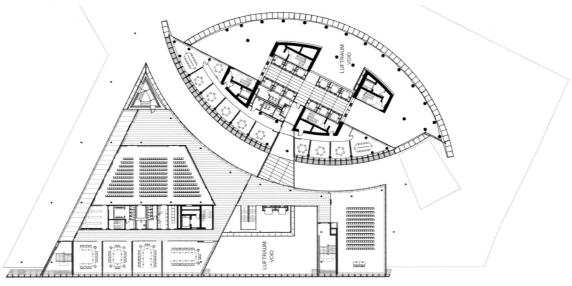

› Ground floor Rez-de-chaussée Erdgeschoss

Sony Center 02

In the reconstruction of Berlin, the Sony Center stands for a new technical vision and order, not being a building, but a part of the city. Surrounding the Sony Center are the traditional urban streets and spaces, inside is a new type of covered, urban Forum for a changing cultural and social interaction of our time. The spatial dynamics and variety is contrasted by a minimalist technological attitude. Light, both natural and artificial, is the essence of the design. The Sony Center is luminous, not illuminated. Façades and roof act as a fabric, which blends natural and artificial light. With its characteristics of transparency, permeability to light, reflection and refraction, there is a constant change of images and effects during day and night, affecting not only the appearance but also maximizing the comfort and providing maximum use of resources.

Au coeur de la reconstruction de Berlin, le Sony Center représente une nouvelle perspective technique. En effet, il ne s'agit pas simplement d'un bâtiment isolé, mais d'un édifice complètement intégré à la ville, puisque le Sony Center est entouré de rues et d'espaces urbains traditionnels. A l'intérieur, il accueille ce nouveau forum urbain couvert dont la conception reflète l'interaction socio-culturelle fluctuante de notre époque. Son dynamisme spatial contraste avec son expression minimaliste et technologique. La lumière est l'essence même de son design. Le Sony Center n'est pas illuminé : il est lumineux. Les façades et la toiture sont à l'image d'une toile qui gère la lumière, artificielle ou naturelle. Fort de sa transparence caractéristique et perméabilité à la lumière, de ses reflets et réfractions, il façonne constamment de nouvelles images, créant des effets diurnes et nocturnes qui, du reste, contribuent à optimiser le confort intérieur avec un minimum de moyens.

Im Rahmen der Neugestaltung des Potsdamer Platzes errichtete man dieses Gebäude, das sich nicht nur völlig in das Stadtbild integriert, sondern auch wie eine Vision der Technik wirkt. Um das Sony Center herum, liegen die alten Straßen und Plätze, während das Innere ein neues, überdachtes städtisches Forum ist, das sich an die sich verändernde soziokulturelle Interaktion der modernen Zeit anpasst. Die räumliche Dynamik und Vielseitigkeit bildet einen Kontrast zu dem minimalistischen und technologischen Bild. Das Licht, sowohl in seiner natürlichen als auch künstlichen Form, ist die Essenz der Gestaltung. Das Sony Center wird nicht beleuchtet, sondern es leuchtet. Fassaden und Dach funktionieren wie ein Gewebe, das das Licht dämpft. Durch diese Transparenz, Reflexe und Lichtbrechungen ändert sich der Gesamteindruck im Tages- und Nachtverlauf, wobei hoher Komfort mit geringem Mitteleinsatz erreicht wird.

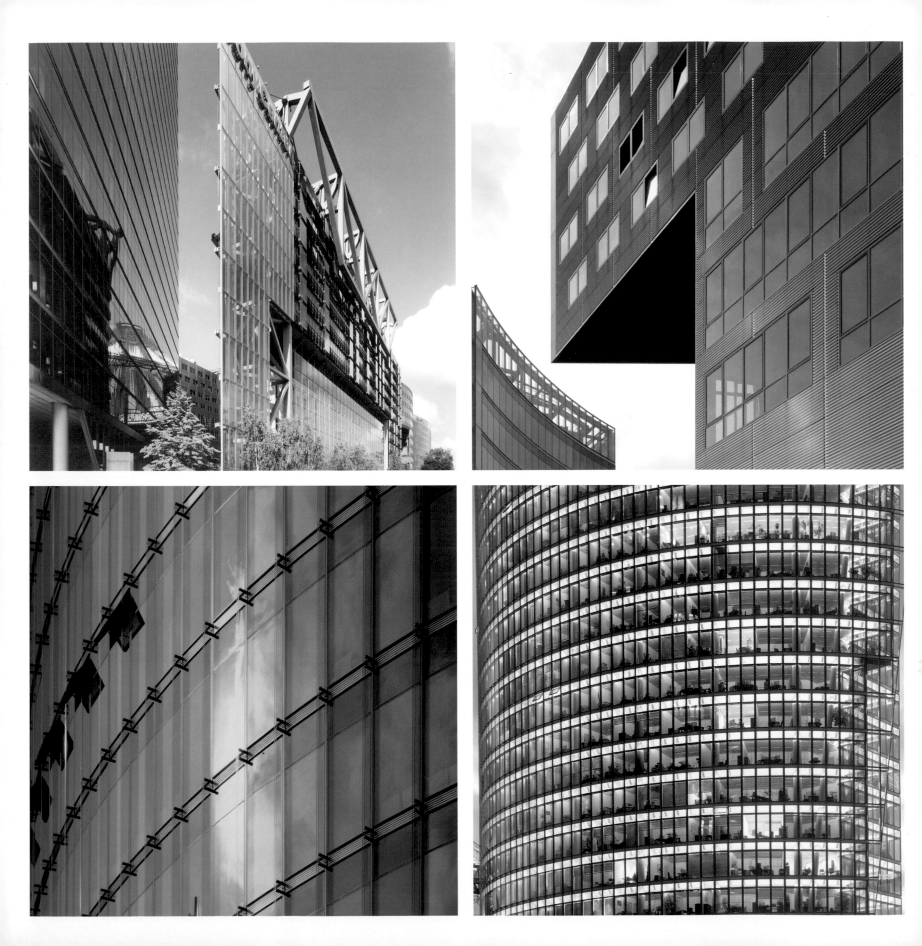

The spatial dynamics and variety of the building along with its – natural or artificial – lighting are the essence of this design.

Son dynamisme spatial, conjuguée à la lumière naturelle ou artificielle, est l'essence même de ce design.

Dynamik, räumliche Vielfalt und Licht, sowohl in seiner natürlichen als auch in seiner künstlichen Form, bilden die Essenz dieser Konstruktion.

› **Sketch** Esquisse Skizze

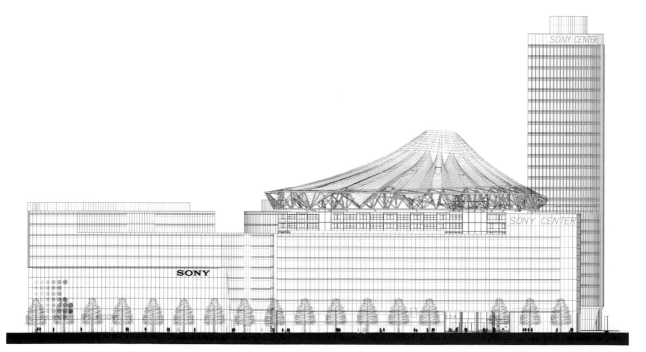

› Elevation Élévation Aufriss

Hesperia Tower

The construction of this hotel was one of the most important interventions in the urban planning program initiated by the City Hall of Hospitalet de Llobregat, intended to transform the skyline and respond to the needs created by the great influx of visitors to this area around a trade fair. The Hesperia Tower, a skyscraper 345 ft and 29 stories in height, stands out on account of the original glass dome situated on its roof terrace. The main façades were conceived as curtain walls with 152 rectangular windows on each façade. This approach is not customary in a hotel, but it has the advantage of providing wide-ranging panoramic views from the interior of the rooms. The only striking touch of color is supplied by the orange window frames, which contrast with the gray of cement and the metal structures of the staircases.

La construction de l'hôtel est une des interventions majeures du programme d'urbanisme de la mairie de l'Hospitalet de Llobregat dont le but est de changer le panorama visuel de la ville et de répondre aux besoins de la clientèle abondante dans cette zone peuplée de salons internationaux. Hesperia Tower est un gratte-ciel de 29 étages, haut de 105 m, qui se distingue par l'originalité de sa structure de verre en forme de coupole située au sommet de la tour. Les façades principales, fortes de 152 fenêtres rectangulaires sur chacune d'elle, sont conçues comme de véritables rideaux muraux : solution inhabituelle pour un hôtel, permettant de jouir d'une immense vue panoramique de l'intérieur des chambres. La seule touche de couleur apparente provient de l'encadrement orangé des fenêtres, contrastant avec le gris propre au béton et aux structures métalliques des escaliers.

Im Rahmen der städtebaulichen Planung der Stadtverwaltung von Hospitalet de Llobregat war die Errichtung dieses Hotels eine der wichtigsten Maßnahmen. Das Stadtbild sollte verändert und verbessert werden und man benötigte Unterkünfte für die Besucher des in der Nähe gelegenen, neuen Messegeländes. Das Hotel Hesperia Tower ist ein 105 m hoher Wolkenkratzer mit 29 Etagen. Es fällt vor allem durch die originelle, kuppelförmige Glasstruktur auf der Dachterrasse auf. Die Hauptfassaden sind als eine Art Gardinen-Wände angelegt. In jeder Fassade befinden sich 152 rechteckige Fenster. Das ist eine außergewöhnliche Lösung für ein Hotel, die es ermöglicht, dass die Gäste aus ihren Zimmern einen weiten Blick über die Stadt haben. Der einzige Farbtupfer an dem Gebäude sind die Fensterrahmen in auffallendem Orange, das einen Kontrast zu dem grauen Beton und den Metallstrukturen der Treppen schafft.

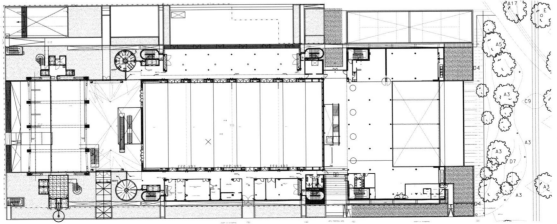

› Plan Plan Grundriss

Evo Restaurant

The Evo restaurant is situated on a circular platform 345 ft high, on top of the 27 floors that comprise the Hesperia Tower Hotel; it appears to be stuck onto the building's rectangular structure, creating a striking geometric contrast. Due to the hotel's distinctive configuration, its interior design had to be both complex and bold. To counterpoint the formal irregularity, circular platforms were created on different levels, adapting to the interior forms by means of ramps and staircases. The huge glass dome, which weighs 115 tons, serves as the roof of one of the latest examples of the designer restaurants that have been enriching the culinary scene in this Catalan city. The architecture combines with the furniture, lighting, atmosphere and colors to establish a harmonious blend of contemporary architecture and the restaurant industry.

Le restaurant Evo est installé sur une plate-forme circulaire, située à 105 m de haut, au sommet des 27 étages qui composent l'hôtel Hesperia Tower. Accolé à la structure rectangulaire de l'édifice, ce bâtiment affiche un contraste géométrique remarquable. Sa configuration particulière engendre un intérieur complexe, mais déterminant. Pour contrecarrer cette irrégularité formelle interne, les architectes ont créé des plateformes circulaires de différentes hauteurs qui épousent les formes intérieures grâce à des rampes ou escaliers. L'énorme coupole de verre, avec ses 115 tonnes, forme la toiture d'un des derniers exemples de restaurants design inscrits au panorama culinaire de la ville catalane. Architecture du local, mobilier, lumières, ambiance ou couleurs sont autant d'éléments qui subliment l'agencement et l'équilibre harmonieux entre concept d'architecture contemporaine et restauration.

Das Restaurant Evo befindet sich auf einer runden Plattform in 105 m Höhe über den 27 Stockwerken des Hotels Hesperia Tower. Die runde Form, die auf der rechteckigen Struktur liegt, lässt einen starken, Kontrast geometrischen entstehen. Aufgrund der besonders auffallenden Gebäudeform war auch eine ausgefallene und komplexe Innengestaltung notwendig. Im Inneren stellte man den unregelmäßigen, äußeren Formen runde Plattformen auf verschiedenen Ebenen entgegen, die über Rampen oder Treppen erreichbar sind. Eine riesige, 115 Tonnen schwere Glaskuppel krönt das Dach dieses modernen Restaurants im avantgardistischen Design, das das kulinarische Panorama der katalanischen Stadt bereichert hat. Sowohl die architektonische Gestaltung als auch das Mobiliar, die Beleuchtung und die Farbgebung vereinen harmonisch das Konzept der modernen Architektur mit der Gastronomie.

In this idyllic setting of panoramic vistas over the city of Barcelona and the sea, one can enjoy exquisite meals.

Dans ce cadre idyllique, façonné par les vues panoramiques surplombant la ville de Barcelone et la mer, on peut savourer des mets délicieux.

In dieser idyllischen Umgebung, mit Blick über die Stadt Barcelona und das Meer, werden ausgezeichnete Gerichte serviert.

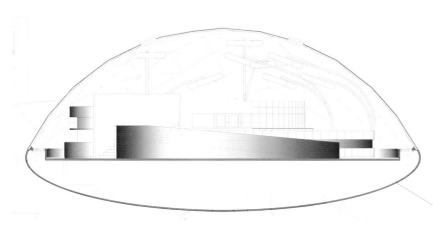

› Section Section Schnitt

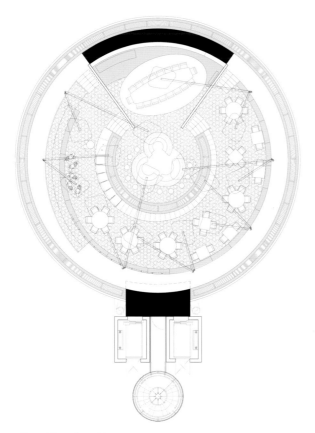

› Plan Plan Grundriss

Due to the particular conditions of the 'UFO's' structure, were chosen, focus lamps projecting light over each table.

Dû aux conditions particulières de la structure de l'«ovni», les lampes sélectionnées diffusent une lumière ponctuelle au-dessus de chaque table.

Aufgrund der speziellen Struktur dieses „UFOs" wählte man Lampen, die Lichtpunkte auf jeden einzelnen Tisch werfen.

The lamps also function as loudspeakers for ambience music, as well as fire extinguishers.

Les lampes servent également de haut-parleurs pour diffuser une musique d'ambiance et même d'extincteurs en cas d'incendie.

Die Lampen dienen dazu noch als Lautsprecher für Hintergrundmusik und schließlich als Feuerlöscher.

Udvar-Hazy Center

The National Air and Space Museum, owned by the prestigious Smithsonian Institution, was built in the 1960s and needed an extension to house its historic collection of air and space machinery. As the project was going to be carried out in Dulles international airport, the architects drew inspiration from an airport terminal for the interior design and the museum was conceived with a structure similar to that of an airport: the space was divided into one earthbound and one aeronautic zone, which also includes the foyer, an IMAX cinema and a conical control tower. The composition also evokes the materials used for aerospace construction, as it incorporates tiles with a metallic look and cladding in the form of shiny, bluish aluminum panels. The exterior façade is strikingly smooth, with straight rectangular windows in some areas.

Le Musée National de l'Air et de l'Espace, datant des années soixante et propriété de la prestigieuse Smithsonian Institution, devait être agrandi pour héberger la collection historique des engins aériens et spatiaux. Face à la nécessité de l'intégrer à l'aéroport international de Dulles, les architectes se sont inspirés d'un terminal pour concevoir l'enveloppe structurelle extérieure du musée, à l'instar d'un aéroport. Les espaces s'articulent autour d'une zone terrestre et aérienne. Cet ensemble inclut un hall, un cinéma IMAX et une tour de contrôle conique. L'édifice est composé de matériaux inspirés des constructions aérospatiales, dans une alliance de carreaux de céramique à l'aspect métallique et de revêtements constitués de panneaux d'aluminium brillants et bleutés. La façade extérieure, parfaitement lisse, affiche par endroits des panneaux de verre droits et rectangulaires.

Das National Air and Space Museum, das zu dem bekannten Smithsonian Institut gehört, stammt aus den Sechzigerjahren und musste dringend erweitert werden, um die historische Sammlung von Maschinen aus der Luft- und Raumfahrt unterzubringen. Da der neue Komplex in der Nähe des Washington Dulles International Airports liegt, ließen sich die Architekten bei der Innengestaltung von einem Flughafenterminal inspirieren. Die Struktur des Museums ähnelt deshalb der eines Flughafens. Die Räume sind in einen Boden- und einen Luftbereich unterteilt. Hinzu kommen die Empfangshalle, ein IMAX-Kino und ein konisch geformter Kontrollturm. Auch die Komposition erinnert an Konstruktionsmaterialien aus der Luft- und Raumfahrt. Es wurden Keramikkacheln mit Metallic-Effekt und Verkleidungen aus glänzenden, bläulichen Aluminiumpaneelen verwendet. Die Fassade ist glatt und teilweise durch geradlinige, rechteckige Fenster unterbrochen.

For better views from all angles the architects designed a series of elevated platforms.

Les architectes ont conçu des passerelles élevées pour obtenir des vues panoramiques de tous les côtés.

Um von allen seiten einen besseren Ausblick zu haben, schufen die Architekten erhöhte Laufstege.

› Elevations Élévations Aufrisse

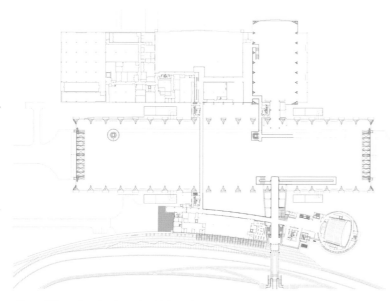

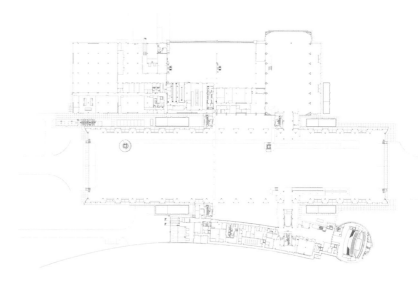

› Ground floor Rez-de-chaussée Erdgeschoss

› First floor Premier étage Erstes Obergeschoss

Burj Al Arab

The Burj al-Arab, located in the largest city of the United Arab Emirates, is marketed as 'the world's first seven-star hotel'. With a height of 1,053 ft, it is the tallest building in the world, used exclusively as a hotel. It stands on an artificial island 919 ft off Jumeirah beach, and is connected to the mainland by a private curving bridge. The hotel was built to resemble the sail of a *dhow*, a type of Arabian vessel. Near the top there is a helipad, and extending from the other side of the hotel, over the ocean, is a restaurant supported by a cantilever. A remarkable element of its architecture is the outer beachward wall of the atrium, made of a woven, teflon-coated fiberglass cloth. The atrium itself is featured as the tallest lobby in the world, designed by the interior designer Khuan Chew.

L'hôtel Burj al Arab, situé dans la ville principale des Emirats arabes unis, s'enorgueuillit d'être le « premier hôtel sept étoiles du monde ». Haut de 321 m, il devient l'hôtel le plus élevé du monde. Situé sur une île artificielle de 280 m face à la plage de Jumeirah, il est relié à la terre ferme par un pont privé aux formes sinueuses. Sa structure est conçue à l'instar d'une voile *dhow*, d'une embarcation arabe. L'édifice accueille un héliport au dernier étage qui se prolonge, de l'autre côté, par un appendice hébergeant un restaurant érigé à l'instar d'une console suspendue. Le mur extérieur de l'atrium est un des éléments les plus remarquables de son architecture, pour être construit à partir d'un tissage de fibres de verre recouvert de teflon. Cet atrium, portant la signature du designer d'intérieur Khuan Chew, passe pour être le vestibule le plus haut du monde.

Das Hotel Burj al Arab in der größten Stadt der Vereinigten Arabischen Emirate wird als das „erste Sieben-Sterne-Hotel der Welt" betrachtet. Mit einer Höhe von 321 m handelt es sich auch um das höchste Hotel der Welt. Es liegt auf einer künstlichen Insel 280 m vor dem Strand Jumeirah und eine kurvige private Brücke verbindet es mit dem Festland. Die Struktur des Gebäudes hat die Form eines Segels eines „Dhau", ein typisch arabischer Segelschiffstyp. Zum Hotel gehört ein Heliport am obersten Stockwerk und ein Restaurant, das auf säulenförmigen Trägern steht. Die Außenmauer des Atriums ist eines der auffallendsten architektonischen Elemente. Sie besteht aus einem Glasfasergewebe, das mit Teflon beschichtet ist. Dieses Atrium, entworfen von dem Innenarchitekten Khuan Chew, gilt als die höchste Empfangshalle der Welt.

With a height of 1,053 ft, the highest hotel in the world is located on an artificial island connected to the mainland by a curving bridge.

Du haut de ses 321 mètres, l'hôtel le plus élévé du monde est situé sur une île artificielle, reliée à la terre ferme par un pont sinueux.

Das 321 m hohe und somit höchste Hotel der Welt, steht auf einer künstlichen Insel, die über eine kurvige Brücke mit dem Festland verbunden ist.

Jumeirah Emirates Towers

Dubai's twin 'Emirates Towers' are deliberately designed to provide an iconic profile, dominating the skyline of the growing business district to the south of the city center. Taller than any other building in Europe and the Middle East at the time of construction, the slightly taller 1,165 ft, 56-story tower houses offices, while the other is mostly a hotel. Clad in aluminum panels with copper and silver reflective glass, the towers capture the changing light of the desert sun and change, depending on the angle of view. To achieve the stability that a high building requires, the architects distributed the structural load at its three farthest corners. But beyond that, the triangle is a form that is evocative of the Islamic culture: in the pattern, the points represent the earth, the sun and the moon.

Les tours jumelles des Emirats, conçues pour devenir l'emblème de Dubayy, surplombent une zone qui s'étend du district commercial en pleine croissance jusqu'au centre urbain. Plus haute que n'importe quel autre édifice d'Europe ou du Moyen Orient lors de sa construction, la tour de 355 m et de 56 étages, un peu plus haute que l'autre, accueille des bureaux, sa jumelle étant avant tout un hôtel. Revêtues de panneaux d'aluminium et dotées de vitres réfléchissantes en cuivre et argent, les tours captent la lumière changeante du désert, modulable selon l'angle de vision. Pour conférer la stabilité nécessaire à un édifice de cette taille, les architectes ont réparti le poids en trois points distincts, formant un triangle qui, outre sa fonction architecturale, représente une forme géométrique évocatrice de la culture islamique, affichant trois points symboliques : la Terre, le Soleil et la Lune.

Die Zwillingstürme Emirates Towers de Dubai, stellen das neue Wahrzeichen der wachsenden Handelsstadt dar und beherrschen diese aus der Höhe. Zur Zeit seiner Errichtung war der höhere der beiden Türme mit 355 m Höhe und 56 Etagen das höchste Gebäude in Europa und im Mittleren Osten. Einer der Türme dient als Bürogebäude, der andere als Hotel. Das Hochhaus ist mit Aluminiumplatten und reflektierendem Glas aus Kupfer und Silber bedeckt. Dieses Dach fängt das wechselnde Licht der Wüste auf, das sich je nach Betrachtungswinkel verändert. Um diesem Gebäude die Stabilität zu geben, die es aufgrund seiner außergewöhnlichen Höhe benötigt, verteilte man das Gewicht auf drei Punkte innerhalb eines Dreiecks. Diese geometrische Form hat nicht nur eine architektonische Funktion, sondern sie spielt auch eine wichtige Rolle innerhalb der islamischen Kultur, da die Spitzen des Dreiecks symbolisch für die Erde, die Sonne und den Mond stehen.

At the time of its construction, the taller of the twin towers was higher than any other building in Europe or the Middle East.

Lors de sa construction, une des deux tours jumelles était alors la plus haute d'Europe et du Moyen Orient.

Im Augenblick der Errichtung war einer der beiden Zwillingstürme das höchste Gebäude in Europa und im Mittleren Osten.

Quai Branly Museum
Musée du Quai Branly
Quai Branly Museum

The architectural concept for this project was based on respect for the environment, both in the choice of materials and in the interaction with the urban landscape of central Paris. The main building of the four comprising this museum complex boasts a long walkway lined with glass and screen prints that is set on top of large pillars above a 4.44-acre garden. A spiral entrance ramp leads inside to a platform with permanent and temporary exhibitions. The museum's layout was conceived as an open platform, where lighting sets up interplay with shadows and the colors are warm and vivid, designed to absorb light. The building's exterior decoration is dominated by earthy shades of brown, black and granite.

Le projet suit un concept architectural respectueux de l'environnement, tant par le choix des matériaux que par l'interaction du paysage urbain du cœur de Paris. L'édifice principal de cet ensemble muséal de 4 bâtiments offre une longue passerelle de verre sérigraphié, surplombant un jardin de 18000 m² juché sur pilotis. Une rampe d'accès en spirale mène à l'intérieur et à la plateforme des collections permanentes et temporelles. L'aménagement intérieur du musée est conçu comme une plateforme ouverte où l'éclairage offre un jeu d'ombres et de lumières, de coloris chauds et intenses, conçus pour absorber la lumière. La décoration extérieure de l'édifice affiche une prédominance de tons sombres, déclinant une palette de grenat, marron, noir et marine.

Bei der Planung dieses Museums sollte vor allem die Umwelt respektiert werden, sowohl in der Auswahl der Materialien als auch in der Interaktion mit der Stadtlandschaft im Herzen von Paris. Der Hauptteil dieses Museumskomplexes, der aus insgesamt vier Teilen besteht, wird von einem langen, von im Siebdruckverfahren bedruckten Glasflächen gesäumten Laufsteg gebildet, der sich auf großen Säulen über einem 18 000 m² großen Garten erhebt. Eine spiralförmige Zugangsrampe führt ins Innere zu einer Plattform, auf der die ständigen Sammlungen und die Zeitausstellungen gezeigt werden. Die Raumaufteilung des Museums beruht auf der Idee einer offenen Plattform, auf der die Beleuchtung mit Schatten und warmen, intensiven Farben spielt, die das Licht absorbieren. An der Fassade des Gebäudes dominieren die Farben Braun, Dunkelrot, Schwarz und Dunkelblau.

The main building consists of a runway built in the shape of an enormous glazed curving wall standing on columns.

L'édifice principal est composé d'une passerelle épousant la forme d'une immense paroi de verre incurvée, hissée sur pilotis.

Das Hauptgebäude besteht aus einer riesigen gekrümmten, verglasten Mauer, die einen Laufsteg bildet und auf Säulen steht.

The highest point of the site displays a series of boxes placed horizontally, and colored in earth, aubergine and ochre tones.

Une rangée horizontale de boîtes peintes dans des tons terre, aubergine et ocre, s'affiche sur le haut de l'enceinte.

Auf dem oberen Teil des Geländes steht eine waagerechte Reihe aus in Erdtönen, Aubergine und Ocker gestrichenen Kästen.

Federation Square

The urban architectural complex of Federation Square was conceived as Melbourne's new, political and cultural center, situated in the heart of the city. On a plot where the constructions have remained virtually intact, the LAB Architecture Studio designed an entire complex that assembles different types of elements and activities while also conserving a formal and visual cohesion. The formal conception sought by the architects was the material and visual coherence of all the buildings, achieved by means of geometrical structures that fit together perfectly through a fractal format. Rectangles and triangles are the geometrical forms most used in the various buildings, while glass, stone and zinc are the predominant materials. The complex also incorporates systems that permit a considerable saving in energy, as in the case of the atrium.

Le Federation Square est un ensemble architectural urbain conçu pour être un nouveau centre social, politique et culturel situé au coeur de Melbourne. Sur un terrain pratiquement dépourvu de toute construction, le LAB Architecture Studio a créé tout un ensemble réunissant éléments et activités de différentes natures dans le respect d'une unité formelle et visuelle. Les architectes ont recherché une conception architecturale qui traduise l'harmonie matérielle et visuelle de tous les édifices par le biais de structures géométriques fractionnées, parfaitement imbriquées l'une dans l'autre. Le rectangle et le triangle sont les formes géométriques les plus récurrentes dans les divers édifices. De même pour le verre, la pierre et le zinc qui sont les matériaux clés de l'enceinte. À cela s'ajoute l'intégration de structures, à l'instar de l'atrium, générant un gain d'énergie considérable.

Die in der Stadtmitte gelegene Gruppe städtischer Gebäude Federation Square bildet das neue soziale, politische und kulturelle Zentrum der Stadt. Auf einem Grundstück, dessen Bauten so gut wie intakt waren, hat das Architekturstudio LAB einen Entwurf umgesetzt, durch den verschiedene Elemente und Aktivitäten vereint werden und der eine visuelle und formale Kohärenz schafft. Das formale Konzept, das die Architekten zu verwirklichen suchten, war es, alle Gebäude durch geometrische Strukturen, die gebrochen und perfekt ineinander gefügt sind, visuell und in ihrem Material zusammenhängend wirken zu lassen. Das Rechteck und das Dreieck sind die beiden geometrischen Formen, die an den verschiedenen Gebäuden überwiegen. Die hauptsächlich verwendeten Materialien sind Naturstein und Zink. Zusätzlich sind Systeme integriert worden, wie z. B. das Atrium, durch die eine beträchtliche Energieeinsparung möglich sind.

Rectangles and triangles are the most used shapes in the various buildings, and glass, stone and zinc are the chief materials employed.

Dans les différents édifices, le rectangle et le triangle sont les formes récurrentes : le verre, la pierre et le zinc en sont les matériaux essentiels.

Rechtecke und Dreiecke sind die geometrischen Formen, die an den Gebäuden überwiegen. Meist wurde Naturstein und Zink verwendet.

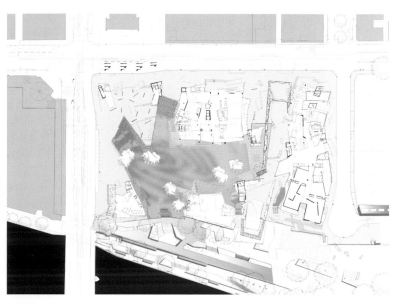

› Location plan   Plan de situation   Umgebungsplan

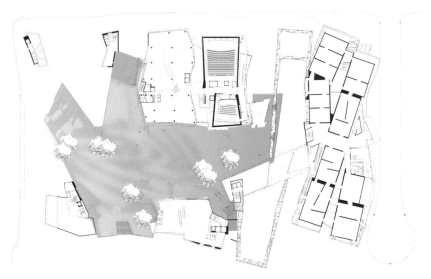

› Location plan   Plan de situation   Umgebungsplan

› Section   Section   Schnitt

› Section   Section   Schnitt

Schlachthausgasse

An open area of approximately 64,500 sq. ft. in the heart of the city came up for development, and the architects in charge of the project suggested erecting two very slim buildings, in line with Schlachtausgasse, in order to conserve most of the valuable trees, giving back to the urban block its original shape. The remaining part of the property was turned into a garden that acts as a sound barrier between the buildings and the noisy street. The complex contains 82 apartments, around 129,000 sq. ft. of office space, as well as an underground parking lot integrated into the side sloping down toward the Danube. The upper part, consisting of 6 + 1 stories, boasts architectural and sculptural elements and perfect distribution, using the interior space most efficiently in terms of natural daylight.

Sur ce terrain d'environ 6.000 m², situé en plein coeur de la ville, les architectes chargés de cette réhabilitation ont proposé, pour conserver au maximum les arbres existants, de construire deux édifices étroits, parallèles à la Schlachthausgasse, restituant ainsi à cet édifice sa forme initiale. Le terrain restant est consacré à un jardin, véritable séparation phonique entre les bâtiments et la très empruntée Schlachthausgasse. Le complexe abrite 82 habitations, environ 12.000 m² d'espace bureaux et un parking souterrain intégré au versant qui donne sur le Danube. La partie supérieure, dotée de 6+1 étages, se distingue par l'émergence d'éléments architecturaux à caractère sculptural et par une distribution parfaite, maximalisant avec efficacité l'espace intérieur au gré des besoins en lumière du jour.

Als ein ungefähr 6 000 m² großes Grundstück im Zentrum der Stadt von Gebäuden frei blieb, schlugen die mit der Neugestaltung beauftragten Architekten vor, die Bäume soweit wie möglich stehen zu lassen, die sich dort befanden. So erbaute man zwei parallele, schmale Gebäude in der Schlachthausgasse, die der Originalstruktur nachempfunden wurden. Auf dem übrigen Grundstück wurde ein Garten angelegt, der die Gebäude akustisch von der belebten Schlachthausgasse isoliert. In dem Gebäude befinden sich 82 Wohnungen, ungefähr 12.000 m² Bürofläche und darunter ein unterirdischer Parkplatz in Richtung Donau. Im Obergeschoss mit 6+1 Etagen fallen insbesondere die skulpturellen, architektonischen Elemente auf, die aus dem Dach herausragen. Die Raumaufteilung optimiert die Nutzung des Innenraums und macht die Räume flexibel. Auch das Tageslicht wird sehr effizient genutzt.

Expo 02

The design concept for Expo 02 was based on the application of urban building strategies focused on the creation of outstanding points of reference in order to establish a basis for future urban development. All the functional elements included in that development plan gave the designers great freedom of action when faced with unexpected changes. The exhibition hall has been designed as a covered platform jutting out over the lake and ending in a space occupied by three towers. With a weight of 350 tons and erected in the shape of an aircraft, these towers stand as symbols of power and freedom. The multipurpose platform, right under the roof of the building, contains the various exhibition pavilions as if they were buildings in a town. Movement and pressure sensors turn the visitors' movements into light and sound reflections, thus interactively shaping the Expo.

Le concept de design pour l'Expo 02 n'est autre que l'application de stratégies de construction urbaine visant à créer des points de référence de nature exceptionnelle, pour servir de base au futur plan de développement urbain. Tous les éléments fonctionnels intégrés dans ce plan accordent aux concepteurs une grande souplesse d'action face à d'éventuels changements. Le salon de démonstration est conçu comme une plateforme couverte qui se projette sur le lac et s'achève en un espace d'où s'élèvent trois tours de 350 tonnes : disposées en forme d'avion, elles symbolisent ainsi le pouvoir et la liberté. La plateforme polyvalente, située sous le toit de l'édifice, abrite les pavillons de l'Expo, comme s'il s'agissait de bâtiments urbains. Les senseurs de mouvement et de pression transforment les déplacements des visiteurs en reflets lumineux et sonores, modulant ainsi la physionomie de l'Expo de manière interactive.

Das Gestaltungskonzept der Expo 02 bestand darin, Strategien im Städtebau so einzusetzen, dass außergewöhnliche Referenzpunkte entstehen, die als Grundlage für die künftige städtische Entwicklung dienen. Alle funktionellen Elemente sind in einen städtischen Entwicklungsplan integriert, der eine flexible Reaktion auf spätere Veränderungen ermöglicht. Das Messegelände wurde als offene Plattform zum See hin angelegt, die in einem Raum mit drei Türmen endet. Diese Türme wiegen 350 Tonnen und ihre flugzeugähnliche Form symbolisiert Kraft und Freiheit. Die überdachte Plattform kann für verschiedene Zwecke genutzt werden. Hier befinden sich die Ausstellungspavillons, so als ob es sich um die Gebäude einer Stadt handelte. Die montierten Bewegungs- und Drucksensoren wandeln die Bewegungen der Besucher in sich verändernde Licht- und Klangreflexe um. So ändert sich auch das Aussehen des Ausstellungsgeländes auf interaktive Weise.

The site of the great exhibition was conceived as a roofed platform jutting out over the lake, ending in the space occupied by the three towers.

L'emplacement de l'exposition est conçu à l'instar d'une plateforme couverte qui s'élance au-dessus du lac pour s'achever en un espace d'où s'élève trois tours.

Das Messegelände wurde als überdachte Plattform angelegt, die sich zum See neigt und auf einem Platz mit drei Türmen endet.

Disney Concert Hall L. A.

Frank O. Gehry's design for the concert hall provides striking evidence of his commitment to creating functional buildings that serve his clients' needs. The original proposal defined the central auditorium as a cluster of intimate boxes opening onto the performance area. This initial design underwent significant modifications as the architect consulted with acoustics experts and prominent classical musicians. Further design produced an auditorium that is shaped like a convex box – bowed in the middle and raised on either end – a structure tailored to convey orchestral sound as effectively as possible. One of the most remarkable details is the effect of crescendos on the external surface of the auditorium, whose rectangular hall has a stainless steel cover which ripples and folds up on its sides.

Le design par Frank O. Gehry de cet auditorium constitue un des exemples les plus éloquents de sa volonté de créer des édifices fontionnels adaptés aux besoins de ses clients. L'idée originale definissait l'auditorium central comme une série de boîtes ouvertes vers la scène. Toutefois, celui-ci a dû subir de profondes modifications, sur les conseils d'acousticiens et d'interprètes renommés consultés par l'architecte en personne. L'architecte a donc construit un nouvel auditorium en forme de boîte afin de renforcer l'acoustique de l'orchestre le plus efficacement possible. Un des détails les plus significatifs est le mouvement sur la superficie des crescendos de l'extérieur de l'auditorium dont la salle rectangulaire est recouverte d'acier inoxydable qui ondule et se rabat sur son pourtour.

Dieses von Frank O. Gehry geplante Auditorium ist eines der besten Beispiele für das Bestreben dieses Architekten, funktionelle Gebäude zu schaffen, die sich an die Notwendigkeiten und Wünsche seiner Kunden anpassen. Die ursprüngliche Idee definierte das zentrale Auditorium als eine Reihe von Kisten, die sich zur Bühne hin öffnen. Der Architekt änderte diesen ersten Vorschlag jedoch stark ab, nachdem er sich mit Experten der Akustik und bekannten Musikern beraten hatte. So entstand ein Auditorium, das die Form einer, in der Mitte zusammengefalteten, konvexen Kiste hat, deren Enden nach oben ragen. Durch diese Form erreichte man eine ausgezeichnete Akustik für das Orchester. Eines der auffallendsten Kennzeichen ist die aufsteigende Bewegung der Flächen an der Fassade. Der rechteckige Saal ist mit Edelstahl verkleidet, der den äußeren Mauern nachzugeben und auf sie zu stürzen scheint.

355

This magnificent building bears Frank O. Gehry's unmistakable stamp.

Le design de cette oeuvre magnifique porte, indubitablement, la griffe de Frank O. Gehry.

Ganz deutlich hinterließ Frank. O. Gehry seine Spuren bei der Gestaltung dieses wundervollen Bauwerks.

The building includes a series of devices that favor rational use of resources through natural light.

L'édifice dispose d'installations favorisant l'usage rationnel des ressources grâce à l'exploitation de la lumière du jour.

Die Installationen im Gebäude sorgen für eine rationelle Verwendung von Ressourcen. So wird zum Beispiel das Tageslicht optimal ausgenutzt.

Inside, a maze of foyers, ramps and galleries encourage human contact and interaction.

À l'intérieur, un labyrinthe de vestibules, rampes et galeries favorise les rencontres, les relations personnelles et les contacts entre les résidents.

Im Inneren ein Labyrinth aus Empfangshallen, Rampen und Galerien, die den Menschen Raum für das Zusammentreffen und die Interaktion bieten.

Guggenheim Bilbao

This building is made up of a series of interconnected volumes, some orthogonal and clad with stone, others curved, twisted and clad with a metallic skin of titanium. These volumes are combined with curtain walls that gives the whole building transparency. The mathematical complexity of the sinuous curves of stone, glass and titanium required computer-aided design. The glass curtain walls were specially treated to prevent sunlight from damaging the artworks inside, while the metal panels, paper-thin, that cover much of the structure like fish scales are made of titanium, a material that also establishes superb conditions for the conservation of artworks. Overall, Gehry's design has resulted in a distinctive, eye-catching and spectacular structure with a sculp-tural presence that acts as a backdrop to the city.

L'édifice affiche une série de volumes interconnectés, certains de forme orthogonale et revêtus de pierre calcaire, d'autres tortueux habillés d'une peau métallique en titane. Ces volumes jouent avec une combinaison de murs-rideaux de verre, dotant ainsi tout l'édifice de transparence. Vu la complexité mathématique de la construction, les courbes sinueuses de pierre, verre et titane ont été créées sur ordinateur. Les rideaux de verre ont reçu un traitement spécial pour que la lumière naturelle n'endommage pas les œuvres. Les panneaux métalliques qui habillent une grande partie de la structure, à l'instar d'« écailles de poisson », sont en lames de titane d'un demi millimètre d'épaisseur, une matière durable extrêmement facile à entretenir. Dans l'ensemble, le design de Gehry forge une structure originale, spectaculaire et particulièrement visible, à l'image d'une sculpture offerte en toile de fond à l'environnement urbain.

Das Gebäude besteht aus einer Reihe von miteinander verbundenen Körpern, manche mit rechtwinkligen Formen und von Kalkstein bedeckt, andere mit gebogenen und gekrümmten Formen, die mit einer Metallhaut aus Titan verkleidet sind. Diese Körper werden mit gläsernen Mauern kombiniert, durch die das gesamte Gebäude sehr transparent wird. Die komplexen gekrümmten Formen aus Stein, Glas und Titan wurden am Computer entworfen. Die Glasmauern wurden nach einem besonderen Verfahren behandelt, damit das Sonnenlicht die Ausstellungsstücke nicht beschädigt, und die Metallplatten, die einen großen Teil der Struktur wie Fischschuppen bedecken, sind Titanstreifen mit einer Dicke von einem halben Millimeter. Dieses Material ist sehr haltbar und kaum pflegebedürftig. Gehry hat eine einzigartige, auffallende und sehr sichtbare Struktur geschaffen, eine bemerkenswerte, skulpturelle Präsenz, ein neuer Hintergrund in der Umgebung der Stadt.

As a whole, Gehry's design forms a distinctive structure, spectacular and eye-catching.

Dans son ensemble, le design de Gehry crée une structure singulière, spectaculaire et particulièrement visible.

Insgesamt schuf Gehry ein einzigartiges, auffallendes und sehr sichtbares Gebäude.

Photo credits   Crédits photographiques   Fotonachweis